52
TRICKS
TO TEACH YOUR DOG

www.DoggieBuddy.com

ISBN-13: 978-0615792590
ISBN-10: 0615792596

www.doggiebuddy.com

Please note that some of these tricks can be damaging if your dog has a history of hip dysplasia or other health concerns. Before attempting any of the tricks in this book, consult your veterinarian as to what is best for your dog.

Published by DoggieBuddy Press

Printed In The United States of America

Dedication

This book is dedicated to Caspian,
our awesome labradoodle

Contents

About DoggieBuddy.com

DoggieBuddy is a free, online resource, created to provide valuable information that every dog owner needs to successfully raise and train a puppy or adult dog.

What do we mean by a free resource? There is an abundance of dog training information on the web, but many are only available through subscription or paid download. We do our best to give you a quality website that is easy to navigate and doesn't require money to access.

Since its beginning in 2007, DoggieBuddy has helped thousands of dog owners in their quest for well-trained, healthy pets.

Our high standard of providing useful information covers a large variety of topics and questions. Quality content is our main focus, and we strive to provide topics that will suit your needs.

For more information, visit www.doggiebuddy.com.

THE PURPOSE OF THIS BOOK

The purpose of this book is to help dog owners gain a better relationship with their pets. With proper care and training, your dog will be happier, and so will you.

Although DoggieBuddy.com provides free instruction for the 52 tricks, this book is meant to be a convenient companion guide to take with you, since the majority of dog training is performed away from a computer.

We hope that this book will help strengthen your relationship with your dog as you work together on these fun exercises.

Before You Begin

I know you are ready to jump on in and start learning how to teach your dog some really fun and interesting tricks, but first there are some things you will need. A lot of the tools required can be found around the house. You don't need special weaving poles or training sticks to teach your dog tricks—you can make your own, and we'll show you how. Below is a basic list of things that you'll need for teaching your dog the 52 tricks found in this book:

Clicker. This is the only thing you'll actually need to purchase. These should be available online or at your local pet-supply store. We sincerely believe that The Clicker Training Method is the easiest way to train your dog. We'll talk more about Clicker Training a bit later.

Touchstick. You don't need to buy a special dog training stick. A simple dowel will suffice, about 36 inches long and 3/8 inches thick. Be sure to use duct tape to generously pad the ends so that your dog will be protected from any sharp edges. A piece of PVC pipe may work just as well.

Treats. You know your dog better than we do, so get some treats you know he'll like. If you train your dog around his dinnertime, you can vary your treats with kibbles.

These are the basic things you need to teach your dog the following tricks. There may also be some other items for specific tricks, household items that should be easily accessible to you. If you have these basic items, you're ready to get started.

1

Respond To The Clicker

This Is The Foundation For All Tricks In This Book

Difficulty	Easy
Prerequisite	None
Items Needed	Clicker, Treats

DoggieBuddy.com recommends Clicker Training for your dog. This is a simple yet highly effective method with the average dog owner in mind. You don't need to know much about dog training to use this method.

Basically, you want to "catch" good behavior with the clicker. What this means is clicking as soon as your dog does a behavior you want. Whenever you click, your dog knows that she will receive a treat, and will do that specific behavior more often. The way we train the dog to respond in this way is simply by clicking and immediately treating the dog. It won't take your dog long to understand that whenever she hears the clicker she'll get a treat. This is an essential step in clicker training your dog. Another term that we will use is "jackpot." This is an extra reward that you give your dog, usually when she has done exceptionally well or performed the trick perfectly for the first time.

Step 1: Click and immediately give your dog a treat.

Step 2: Repeat about 30 times. This teaches your dog to associate the click with the treat.

Step 3: To maintain this connection, it is important to follow the rule: Never click without treating and never treat without first clicking (we have one exception to this important rule in the Come command - Trick #8).

OUR EXPERIENCE

When I taught my dog Caspian to respond to the clicker, I did it over several training sessions. By the end of each five-minute session, he would always jerk his head toward me when he heard the sound of the clicker. Of course, I gave him several training sessions to reinforce his learning, but dogs catch on to this quickly.

> **TIP:** *"After a while, your dog will stop what he is doing and immediately come to you for a treat. Because of this, you might be tempted to use the clicker to get your dog to come to you. Don't use the clicker in this way. The clicker is meant to shape behavior, and using it as a recall device might teach your dog to run away or behave opposite your intentions."*

TEACHING TROUBLE

Where Can I Find More Info On This Method?

Renowned dog trainer Karen Pryor has several books on the Clicker Training Method, which are great resources for any dog trainer, experienced or not.

For more information about how clicker training works, who invented it, the pros and cons, visit our website: www.doggiebuddy.com.

2

Teach Your Dog Its Name

Yes, A Dog Needs To Be Taught Its Name!

Difficulty •• Easy
Prerequisite •••••••••••••••••••••••••••••••••••••• None
Items Needed •••••••••••••••••••••••••••••••• Clicker, Treats

After teaching your dog to respond to the clicker, you are now ready to use it to teach him many tricks and commands. Throughout this book, we demonstrate how the clicker can be used for both basic commands and more advanced tricks. If you want a well trained dog, one of the first things you need to teach is the most basic of commands: his name.

Step 1: Ignore your dog until he looks directly at you. Click and treat.

Step 2: Do this several times, eventually adding your dog's name right before you click and treat.

Step 3: Continue doing this until your dog will look at you when you say his name.

OUR EXPERIENCE

With Caspian, I grabbed my clicker and tore some bacon into small pieces. The first thing that Caspian needed to know was that whenever he looked at me, I would click and he could get a piece of bacon. I started out just ignoring Caspian and all he was doing. He looked down for a minute, exasperated, and then back up at me. Suddenly, he heard a click, and a treat dropped to the ground. A bit surprised (and grateful), he immediately swallowed it and looked up again. CLICK! I threw it a bit farther away this time so he had to turn around. When he got his treat, he turned around to look at me, and I clicked and treated again. By this time I had started saying his name whenever he looked at me. "Caspian," click, treat.

> **TIP:** *"Always end before your dog gets tired. You want your dog to look forward to his training session. Sessions are more productive when they enjoy it."*

Soon, I knew he was getting the idea of what was going on. I waited until he looked away and I said, "Caspian." He jerked his head over toward where I was sitting and I clicked and treated, giving him a big piece of bacon.

TEACHING TROUBLE

Why doesn't he remember tricks?

Even though Caspian had learned his name by the end of the session, I continued to have training sessions with him just to reinforce the trick. It's so easy for a dog to learn a trick and do it every time today, but tomorrow it may be forgotten. We need to also train in different environments so that our dog won't associate the trick with a particular place. If we are patient and stick with it, our dogs will do the same and will eventually obey us every time.

3

Teach Your Dog Touch

*Teach Your Dog To Touch The End Of A Wooden Dowel,
A Foundation Many Tricks Build Upon*

Difficulty •• Easy
Prerequisite •• None
Items Needed •••••••••••••••••••••• Clicker, Treats, Wooden Dowel

In this next trick, you will teach your dog to touch the end of a "Touchstick." This is just a wooden dowel that's around 36 inches long and 3/8 inches thick. I recommend putting duct tape around the ends to protect your dog from any sharp edges. Wind the tape around and around the ends so that it pads the ends of the stick. With the touchstick, you will be able to teach many of the other tricks in this book, so learning this right away is essential for your dog.

Step 1: Hold your touchstick away from you, offering it to your dog, and wait.

Step 2: Dogs are naturally curious, so when your dog touches it with his nose or mouth, click and treat. Keep doing this until he starts touching the stick without hesitation. If he isn't curious about the touchstick, gently tap his nose and click at the same time.

Step 3: Next time he touches the stick, click and treat, giving the command, "Touch" at the same time.

Step 4: When he can touch the stick on command, give him a jackpot, and make sure to praise him for his good work.

OUR EXPERIENCE

When I taught Caspian to touch the stick, I started out by holding it away from myself and waiting on him to decide what to do. He stared at it for a while, but finally, he curiously touched the end of it with his nose. I clicked immediately and gave him a treat. After doing this a few times, Caspian started touching without hesitating. He knew he'd get a treat if he touched the stick. By this point I started saying, "Touch!" when his nose touched the end of the stick. After several times doing this, he was able to touch the stick at the command. A few more sessions perfected this trick, and I have been able to use it as a foundation for many other tricks!

TEACHING TROUBLE

My Dog Is Touching The Wrong Part of the Stick!

When Caspian started touching the middle of the stick rather than the tip, I just ignored him. Of course, he thought he deserved a treat and started growling at me. I said nothing and ignored him. If I rewarded him for touching the wrong part of the stick, this trick wouldn't be as effective in teaching Caspian other tricks. Finally Caspian decided he should try something else and moved his nose on down to the tip. As soon as his nose touched the taped part of the stick, I clicked and treated.

> **TIP:** *"When making your touchstick, make sure that the ends are covered to protect your dog from injury. You can cover the end of the dowel with layers of duct tape or other soft covering."*

4

Teach Your Dog To Sit

An Essential Command That Every Dog Should Know

Difficulty	Easy
Prerequisite	None
Items Needed	Clicker, Treats

Teaching your dog to sit is one of the most basic commands to teach your dog. Since sitting is such a natural action that your dog does hundreds of times each day, this trick is best "caught" with the clicker. In other words, have your clicker handy, and be on the lookout for your dog to sit. When she does, be ready to immediately click and treat. Timing is essential to catching behaviors with the clicker; click too early or too late, and you might be rewarding a behavior different than the one you want. Timing your clicks just takes a little bit of practice, but once you get the hang of it, it's an amazing tool to use for training your dog. Have fun clicking!

Step 1: Wait until she sits down on her own. Click and treat.

Step 2: Repeat several times.

Step 3: Say Sit as soon as she sits. Click and treat.

Step 4: Repeat several times.

Step 5: Say Sit. If she sits, click and give her a jackpot. If she does not, return to Step 3.

OUR EXPERIENCE

This was the very first trick we taught Caspian. We were so anxious to begin training him, we had barely gotten him home be-

fore we were clicking and treating. Our poor dog was so tired from an all day flight just to get to us, but he had enough energy to try this trick a few minutes before falling asleep. We had no trouble teaching Caspian this command. He was obediently sitting within just a few minutes.

TEACHING TROUBLE

My dog doesn't know what to do!

Be patient with her if she starts barking or whining. Ignore the behavior and wait. You sometimes have to be very patient when clicker training your dog. If your dog gets frustrated, wait until she sits, click and treat well, and take a break. It is better to have short productive training sessions with lots of breaks than long unfruitful sessions.

> **TIP:** *"A good idea is to teach this trick in a small room, such as a bathroom. Because of the small space, dogs are more likely to sit faster."*

5

Teach Your Dog Down

Use This Trick To Build More Advanced Tricks

Difficulty	Easy
Prerequisite	Touch
Items Needed	Clicker, Treats, Touchstick

All you need to teach your dog to lie down is some space, a clicker, and a good treat. Once you have what you need, go ahead and give your dog a small whiff of the treat to get him going. Sometimes this is an easy way to get your dog to try to figure out ways to get more treats.

Method One: "Catch" the behavior

Step 1: Grab your clicker and a good treat.

Step 2: Just watch your dog and wait for him to lie down. When he lies down, immediately click and treat.

Step 3: Keep waiting for your dog to do it again. Soon he will realize that he gets a click and treat whenever he lies down.

Step 4: When your dog begins to lie down more often, add the command and say "Down" when you click.

Step 5: After repeating a few more times to reinforce the action, say, "Down." If the dog lies down at the command, give him a jackpot for his good work!

Method Two: "Lure" the behavior

Step 1: Tell your dog to sit.

Step 2: From the sitting position, lure the dog forward and down using the touch-stick (see illustrations).

Step 3: Click and treat when he is in the down position.

OUR EXPERIENCE

The treat I used is just a slice of American cheese. It digests well for dogs, and Caspian really enjoys it. At first, of course, Caspian didn't know what to do. Since we were training outside, all the sounds and smells of neighborhood activities got in the way. I had to call him back to me a few times when he got distracted. But the treat I had for him was good and, of course, Caspian is eager to do anything for a good treat.

TIP: *"It could take several training sessions for you to perfect a trick. Make sure you don't wear your dog out. Give him plenty of breaks. Always end on a good note and you will never go wrong."*

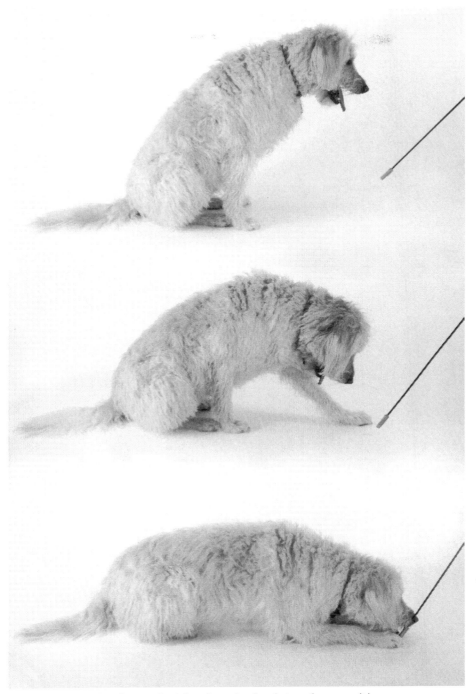

Use the touchstick to lure the dog into a down position

TEACHING TROUBLE

My dog won't lie down when I tell him to!

Make sure you keep your training sessions short. If you go too long, your dog will get tired and stop cooperating. Also, he may not understand the command. In this case, take a break and come back later. Once he's rested and excited to work again, give him the command. If he still does not lie down start the steps over. Make sure you use his favorite treats so he's eager to cooperate. Remember, short sessions! You want to keep it fun and interesting.

6

Teach Your Dog To Stand

Grooming And Care Is Much Easier If Your Dog Will Stand Still

Difficulty •• Easy
Prerequisite •••••••••••••••••••••••••••••••• Down or Sit
Items Needed •••••••••••••••••••••• Clicker, Treats, Touchstick

Now that your dog knows how to "Sit" and "Lie Down," a good command to teach next is "Stand." This command is more helpful than novel. Keep in mind, since standing is such a normal thing for your dog it may be difficult for him to understand why he is being rewarded. Sometimes it helps to click him as he stands up from a sitting or lying position. This will help him realize that it is the standing up action you are looking for.

Step 1: Have your dog lie down. Wait for him to stand up, or use the touchstick to lure him into standing (don't let him touch the stick, click when he stands). When he stands up, click and treat. Repeat this action several times until he learns that he has to stand up in order to get his treat. Standing is so natural that it is likely that the dog won't immediately understand why he is being rewarded, so it may take more repetition than usual. (Initially, it's okay to click even if he isn't standing perfectly; you can work up to this gradually.)

Step 2: Begin to introduce a visual cue (like your hand gesturing upward) and a verbal command ("Stand") so that he can associate those with standing. Click and treat.

Step 3: Have him lie down, then say, "Stand." Jackpot when he stands in the perfect position on command.

TIP: *"Try to keep commands to one or two-syllable words. These are easiest for dogs to identify."*

OUR EXPERIENCE

When Caspian learned to stand, I started out having him lie down. I waited until he stood up. While he was standing up, I clicked and treated. Doing this several times, he soon learned that he had to stand up to get a treat. I started using my command (Stand!) as I had him stand up. Soon, he would stand up when I gave the command. I did this in other sessions in Down positions as well as Sitting, Playing Dead, etc., to give him different scenarios for his new trick.

TEACHING TROUBLE

My dog doesn't want to stand up once he's down!

If you've followed the steps correctly, the thing to do now is make sure you keep your dog interested and willing to cooperate. In other words, make sure he's excited! If he is bored with the treats, grab a tennis ball or a favorite toy. When he sees it he'll most likely jump up and want to play. Don't give it to him yet. Have him sit or lay down and then give him the command to Stand. When he cooperates, treat him with the toy and give it a good throw. Again, the key to a successful training session is to keep things fun and interesting.

7

Teach Your Dog Release

This Command Tells Your Dog To Be Released From Sitting Or Staying

Difficulty •••••••••••••••••••••••••••••••••••••• Easy
Prerequisite •••••••••••••••••••••••••••••• Down or Sit
Items Needed •••••••••••••••••••••••••••• Clicker, Treats

A good command to teach next is "Release." This is much easier to teach if your dog consistently sits on command and stays. This is a dog-training essential, a way to tell your dog that it's okay to move around freely. For example, when your dog is playing with a toy, you can have him "Sit" or "Lie Down" and then toss the toy. Your dog should remain in the sitting or down position until the "Release" command is given.

Step 1: Give the command to "Sit." After waiting five to eight seconds, go ahead and use the vocal command with a hand motion of your choice to tell your dog to be released from his sitting position. If you act excited while doing this, your dog should naturally release. When he does so, click and treat. Repeat this step until your dog is consistently releasing.

Step 2: Eventually, you will want to be less enthusiastic with your command and will want your dog to release when given a more subtle cue. To do this, again give the command to "Sit." After your dog holds for 5-8 seconds, use just the vocal command, but still be just as energetic as before. Each time you repeat this, you'll want to tone down your enthusiasm a little at a time to make the command more subtle.

Step 3: In subsequent sessions, extend the wait time (about 4 or 5 seconds per session) before giving the release, gradually building up endurance so that your dog will wait several minutes before being released.

OUR EXPERIENCE

When teaching Caspian to release from a sitting or down position, we used the term "Go" as our release command. Playing fetch is Caspian's all time favorite thing to do, and we will usually run through several tricks before throwing the ball. This is a good command for us to use to tell him that his patience has paid off, and he can now run after the ball.

> **TIP:** *"Be enthusiastic as much as you can to help your dog learn this trick!"*

TEACHING TROUBLE

My dog releases before I tell him to!

This is a common problem that is easy to fix. What might be happening is your dog senses the amount of time between when you give him the command to sit (or lie down) and when you give him the command to release. Try varying the time between the two commands. Try giving him the release command after 3 seconds, then give him the command after 5 seconds the next time. Another thing that may be happening is that your dog is responding to a visual cue that you aren't aware of. Dogs are smart creatures, and can respond to facial expressions and very slight movements. You might be giving him a cue to release and not even know it!

8

Teach Your Dog Come

This Is Perhaps The Most Important Command You Can Teach Your Dog

Difficulty •• Moderate
Prerequisite •• Down or Sit
Items Needed •••••••••••••••••••••••••••••••••••••• Clicker, Treats

If you only teach your dog one thing from this book, teach him this command—it could save his life. If your dog will not always come when called, he is not safe off leash. Teaching your dog to come when called is not only valuable for your dog's safety but also makes spending time with your dog more enjoyable knowing that he will not cause trouble by running away. If you teach your dog to come when called, and practice it every day, then you will build a trusting relationship with your dog.

Step 1: Load the cue instead of the clicker. Here's how:
Go up to your dog and give the command that you will use to call the dog, then treat him. For example: Say, "Here Max!" and give him a piece of bacon. Repeat multiple times during the day and each time give different treats (bacon, chicken, kibble, tug game; but in addition to treats, always give praise).

Step 2: Go across the room and give the command, "Here Max!" He will come to you to get his treat. When he does, click and jackpot (give a large treat or several treats). At this point in the training go back to click treating when he comes.

Step 3: Each time your dog comes to you pet his head and loop your hand under his collar before you give the treat. This is to get your dog used to being held when he comes to you. Dogs will pull away if they think they are being cornered into something they would rather not be doing. This should be a habit for you as well as the dog.

Step 4: Try calling him from different rooms.

Step 5: Practice calling him when he is interested in something else. Vary the reward each time: sometimes a treat, sometimes just praise.

> **TIP:** *"Get your family or friends to help you out. Have someone call your dog. If he comes to that person, treat. If he comes to someone else, be still and quiet until he finds the person who called him."*

OUR EXPERIENCE

Caspian is a really smart labradoodle, but the one thing that was not good at was coming when he was called. He got excited extremely easily and lost focus during training sessions if he saw other dogs or other activity going on. Truthfully, we were simply irresponsible in teaching him such an important command. One day, after playing fetch outside in our field, he spotted a squirrel, and took off after it. We tried calling him back to us, but he was too interested in the animal he was chasing. They ran across a road at the same time a car was coming down the mountain. The driver didn't have time to stop and hit Caspian going around 30 miles per hour. Caspian rolled about fifty feet, knocking down a construction sign next door. We rushed him to the emergency veterinarian, who wasn't extremely hopeful. Caspian didn't have any broken bones but couldn't move his back legs. It was a long road to recovery, but after several days, the swelling on his spinal cord decreased, and he was able to stand for a few seconds at a time. After many weeks of working with him, he was able to move around like he used to, but not quite as limber. And, even today he carries scars from skidding along the pavement. That experience taught us that teaching the recall command, teaching "Come," is more important than anything else we could teach our dog.

TEACHING TROUBLE

I've taught my dog "Come" before, but now he won't obey me.

We originally taught Caspian to "Come" as a puppy by playing a game where several people stood in a circle taking turns calling the dog and Caspian would come to each person calling him to get a treat. Unfortunately, later we poisoned the "Come" command by using it primarily to go in the house after a play time - he started to associate the command with not being able to play anymore. We decided to start over and teach him using a different command word (we used "here").

9

Teach Your Dog Stay

A Simple Command That Tells Your Dog To Stay Put

Difficulty •• Easy
Prerequisite •• None
Items Needed •••••••••••••••••••••••••••••••••• Clicker, Treats

Company arrives, and your dog goes wild. You can't keep him away from them; sniffing, nudging, licking. If only he knew to stay when you told him, to keep a good distance between himself and your company.

You seat yourself at the dining table. The meal is laid out before you, its scent rising around you, ice cold tea poured in the glass next to the salad bowl, and beside you hangs your dog's dripping tongue and his eyes pierce you in want of the food you have yet to taste.

You tell him to get out. He does, but not allowing quite enough time to let you sip your tea, or take a bite, or say a word to your dinner guest as he unfolds a dark-red napkin onto his lap. The dog is back; you give him nothing. He trots past you and lays his large muzzle on top of the black suit pants of your guest, onto his red napkin, stares into his eyes, towards his plate, again into his eyes.

He comes and he goes, and he comes. Lock him outside on the screened-porch? He'll only bark. Loudly. You'll force him out of the room, but he won't stay even if you tell him to. He doesn't know how. You haven't trained him.

Although teaching your dog to sit or lie down should keep him in that position until you give the release command, it is sometimes helpful to have a "Stay" command for longer periods of waiting, or if you want your dog to freeze in the middle of an action.

Step 1: Have your dog sit.

Step 2: Say "Stay." Wait six seconds. Say "Release" then click and treat.

Step 3: Say "Sit," "Stay" and wait ten seconds. Say "Release" then click and treat.

Step 4: Repeat four or five times per session.

Step 5: Practice this trick in multiple sessions every day, gradually building up to several minutes before releasing.

> **TIP:** *"Make sure your dog is staying still as a statue until you say release."*

OUR EXPERIENCE

We don't usually use the stay command with Caspian, unless we want to emphasize that we want him to freeze and not move. We tell him to stay when we balance a treat or toy on his nose before giving him a release command to catch it. In addition to using the clicker, we would physically restrain him by holding his collar. We would gradually lessen our hold each time until he would stay on his own. We did this because Caspian gets excited easily, and will sometimes "jump the gun" so to speak.

TEACHING TROUBLE

My dog is so impatient!

Dogs are impatient, it's true. You have him sit, you tell him to stay, but he might have other ideas. You haven't quite reached the ten second mark, and he's running towards you. He's impatient and wants a treat now. He knows that sooner or later he'll get it, and he prefers sooner.

Sometimes, the dog owners are the ones who are impatient. You tell your dog to stay, but he won't stay so you get frustrated. But screaming at your dog won't help. In order for a dog to "Stay," patience must be put to order, for both the dog and his owner. Go over the steps, and soon you're dog will get the message. Don't relent if they come begging before you reach your set time limit, and don't treat them. You might have to go back a few seconds, or even half a minute. But make sure your dog is staying still as a statue until you say "Release."

10

Teach Your Dog Heel

Teach Your Dog To Walk Beside You Without Pulling At His Leash

Difficulty ••••••••••••••••••••••••••••••••••••••• Easy
Prerequisite •••••••••••••••••••••••••••••••••••• None
Items Needed •••••••••••••••••••••••••••••• Clicker, Treats

For a well-trained dog, teaching heel—to walk beside you with a loose leash without pulling—is a must. Consider these two examples:

A man opens his front door and exits with his dog on leash. It is a busy neighborhood. Other dogs bark around him, cars whoosh down the road through puddles of rain. The soggy ground is imprinted with his footprints and exactly next to them are his dog's. As if glued to his side the dog trots. Never venturing ahead. Never falling behind to sniff at a mysterious stump or for whiff of a bush that rumors another dog's scent. The leash dangles in a calm arch.

Across the street a woman yells. The man stops to watch, the dog with him. She is flung forward clinging to a black leash. A small dog runs ahead pulling her where it wishes to sniff. The man grins, then laughs aloud.

Step 1: Begin by having your dog on a leash looped to your belt on your left side. That way you don't have to use your hands to hold the leash.

Step 2: Should your dog pull on the leash, never go in the direction that your dog is pulling.

Step 3: When your dog is close to you with his shoulder by your left leg, then click and treat. (If you are walking you will have to stop to treat. That's ok, using the clicker in this way greatly speeds up the time it takes for your dog to learn this important skill.)

Step 4: When your dog starts walking regularly by your left side, begin using the commands "Let's go" and "With me" so that the dog will associate those commands with that position by your side. These commands are more natural than saying "Heel."

Step 5: Click and treat every ten steps that your dog completes by your left side.

Step 6: Work in 10 to 15 minute sessions about four times each day until the skill is mastered.

Step 7: When your dog is faithfully responding to the "Let's go" and "With me" commands by walking by your side, then begin off leash training.

OUR EXPERIENCE

Caspian was only a puppy when we first started working on this. To go outside was a new adventure for him every time, and he would want to check out everything. Even though he was just a puppy, he pulled quite hard on the leash and would end up choking himself. If I ran with him, he would see the leash as a toy, and jump up to catch it. He would hold the leash in his mouth, like he was "taking his human on a walk," instead of the other way around. Although we started with these difficulties, it didn't take too long for him to understand that I was in charge. Consistency cured his pulling problem.

> **TIP:** *"Start by teaching off leash tricks in a fenced-in yard or enclosed area so that you don't lose your dog."*

TEACHING TROUBLE

He just won't listen!

Dogs are sometimes obstinate. If they want to pull you on the leash in order to get somewhere faster, they will. The main rule for you in training your dog to heel is for you to be firm and obstinate yourself. Never go in the direction that your dog is pulling. If anything, go the opposite direction that your dog wants to go and train him to always walk by your side. Just a few steps of walking right next to you are great strides toward your goal. Remember to click and treat well and only do ten or fifteen minutes of training at a time.

11

Teach Your Dog Take It

This Command Tells Your Dog To Pick Up An Item You Point To

Difficulty •• Easy
Prerequisite ••• Touch
Items Needed •••••••••••••••••••••••••••••••• Clicker, Treats, Dog Toy

Congratulations! Your dog should be behaving very well now, having mastered the basics (basic yes, but tricks #1-10 are the most important things your dog can learn). Now, let's work on training your dog to properly interact with the world around him. One of the great things about dogs is their ability to help others, and being able to pick up dropped items or other objects is a very practical thing for dogs to do. In fact, assistance dogs are trained to do this very thing. Whether or not that is your goal, teaching your dog "Take it" is a very beneficial trick which we will build off of later on.

Step 1: Get one of your dog's favorite toys and set it on the ground. Wait for him to pick it up in his mouth. Click and treat.

Step 2: Repeat this several times. When he starts picking up the toy without hesitation, start using the command "Take it" when you click and treat.

Step 3: After a few times of that, see if he will pick it up at your command.

Step 4: See how many objects he'll pick up! Point to the sock and say, "Take it." Click and treat. Point to the remote and say "Take it," etc.

OUR EXPERIENCE

It wasn't hard to teach Caspian "Take it." I set down a toy he really loves and waited to see what he would do. He looked around to figure out what was going on and saw the toy there. He bent down to chew on it and I clicked and treated. I did this again, each time waiting a bit longer to teach him that I wanted him to keep it in his mouth until I clicked. After a while I started using the command "Take it" when he got it right.

> **TIP:** *"Teaching your dog "Take it" will pave the way for many great tricks later on!"*

TEACHING TROUBLE

He gets frustrated and won't pick it up!

Believe it or not, he may be getting frustrated because you are! Do your best to be patient and don't say anything. If your dog growls, ignore him. He'll eventually get it. You may need to click for any behavior that is not quite but close to what you want (i.e., if he goes near the object or touches it). After that, you can eventually shape it into the behavior you want.

12

Teach Your Dog Leave It

Not Just A Trick, This Command Can Save Your Dog's Life

Difficulty ••••••••••••••••••••••••••••••••••••••• Easy
Prerequisite •••••••••••••••••••••••••••••••••••• Touch
Items Needed •••••••••••••••••••••••••• Clicker, Various Treats

The man pats the dog next to him, "She's heeling fine," he says out loud, "Good girl, Daisy, good girl." He peers hard into the night; the wind stings his ears in a chilling burst; the flashlight clicking on, though weakly revealing the terrain before him in its dim gaze: nothing two double-A batteries couldn't fix, if only he had some extras.

He rounds the house's corner and makes for the woods behind the house. He yawns. It's late in the night. He would be asleep by now if only his dog would have eaten at proper hours and not at bedtime. He passes close by the neighbor's house, pulls Daisy away from their compost pile with a gentle tug on the leash.

"Why do they have to dump their dinner leftovers there?" he asks to himself. He looks down. She had snatched a long chicken bone, and she was about to bite down on it.

"Leave it!" he commands. She drops it immediately. He sighs, relieved.

Whether it is a chicken bone that can splinter and choke your dog, a sock which you don't want to have to replace, or any other item you don't want your dog to pick up, this is another command that can potentially save your dog's life.

Step 1: With your dog on a leash, let her smell the dog biscuit, then drop it two or three feet in front of her.

Step 2: Call her by name and say "Leave it" as she starts for the treat. Restrain her with the leash.

Step 3: When your dog looks at you, click and treat with the chicken cube. Praise her as she gives up the dog biscuit for the chicken cube treat.

Step 4: Repeat steps 1-3 five times the first session.

Step 5: In your next session, repeat steps 1-4, but use part of a hot dog as the bait and liver as the reward.

Step 6: In subsequent sessions, teach "Leave it" as above, training off-leash in a fenced yard.

Step 7: Regularly call your dog away from things that she likes: other dogs, treats etc., and then let her go back after you have praised her.

OUR EXPERIENCE

After teaching Caspian this incredibly useful command, we would regularly use the "Leave it" command when outside with him. One day, I had him out off leash, playing fetch with a tennis ball. My neighbor was out, spraying around and old stump with some poison. Caspian was interested in what he was doing, and went to investigate. "Leave it," I said. Caspian immediately turned and came back to me. My neighbor looked up and said, "That's the smartest dog!"

TEACHING TROUBLE

My dog won't leave the treat, even for a better one!

Make sure your dog knows you have an even better treat. And, again, be patient. It is worth it to spend extra time on this trick, because it might save your dog's life!

> **TIP:** *"Be consistent with your dog! Let her know that whenever she leaves something, she will receive something better in return."*

13

Teach Your Dog Bring It

This Command Tells Your Dog To Bring You An Object

Difficulty ••••••••••••••••••••••••••••••••••••• Easy
Prerequisite •••••••••••••••••••••••••••••••• Take It
Items Needed ••••••••••••••••••••••• Clicker, Treats, Toy

"Bring it" is a staple for dog training which we'll use to build other tricks upon. For example, after you teach your dog "Bring it," it will be easy to teach him to fetch, bring his dish or leash, or teach funnier tricks like "Bring me a drink" (Trick #46) or "Get me a tissue!" (Trick #47.)

Step 1: Tell your dog to get a toy by using the "Take it" command.

Step 2: Encourage your dog to come towards you with the toy. Click and treat if he brings it towards you a few steps. Do this a few times.

Step 3: Keep encouraging him to come nearer to you with the toy. Click and treat when he comes to you with the toy.

Step 4: Repeat these steps until your dog brings the toy to you each time without much prompting. Use the command "Bring it!" as you teach.

Step 5: Put the toy on the ground and walk across the room. Say, "Take it" and "Bring it!" If your dog obeys, click and give him a jackpot!

OUR EXPERIENCE

I put Caspian's toy on the floor, saying, "Take it!" He grabs it and looks at me. I pat my leg to encourage him to come to me. Immediately, he takes several steps toward me. I click and treat. We do this several times; each time Caspian gets closer to me. One time he drops the toy and comes to me. I ignore him. Now he is bringing me the toy every time. I click and treat, saying "Bring it" when he comes with the toy. Soon Caspian was able to understand my command and bring me the toy whenever I asked him.

> **TIP:** *"Practice with different objects in different rooms, and have other people help you out by giving your dog the command themselves!"*

TEACHING TROUBLE

He'll come to me just fine, but without the toy!

Don't click and treat when he comes to you without the toy - that's not what you're trying to teach. Be kind, but tough! Begin by clicking if he moves towards your direction with the toy in his mouth. Soon your dog will understand he has to bring it to you!

14

Learn Names

Teach Your Dog The Names Of Household Objects

Difficulty ●●●●●●●●●●●●●●●●●●●●●●●●●●●●●●●● Moderate
Prerequisite ●●●●●●●●●●●●●●●●●●●●●●●●●●●●●●●●●● Touch
Items Needed ●●●●●●●●●●●●●●●●●●●●●●●●●●●●● Clicker, Treats

Dogs are a lot smarter than we give them credit for and can learn the names of all sorts of things. A border collie named Chaser currently holds the record for the largest dog vocabulary, having learned the names of over 1000 different toys and items. Dogs aren't limited to objects, they can learn the names of people and other pets as well. Wouldn't it be nice if your dog knew your kids' names? You can teach your dog the names of all his toys, the remote, or a place like his kennel or the living room.

Step 1: Have your dog touch your hand and click treat.

Step 2: Hold the object in your hand and say touch. Click and treat when he touches the object, not when he touches your hand.

Step 3: Call the object by its name (tug, squeaky, bunny, etc.) just as he touches it. Click and treat.

Step 4: Hold the object and say its name and click and treat when he touches it.

Step 5: For teaching the names of people (Bob, Joe, Dad, Mom, etc.) and places (bed, corner, kennel, etc.) use the touchstick to introduce the person or place (See "Go to a place," Trick #20).

OUR EXPERIENCE

I started out by waiting until Caspian looked at his toy, "Bobo." I clicked and treated. I did this several times until he was looking at it often. This got his attention and directed it toward Bobo. Then, I only started clicking and treating when he went toward the toy and touched it. Each time he touched it with his mouth (or paw, whichever you prefer), I would click and treat. Soon, he did it so often that I started saying "Bobo" whenever he touched it. Now, when I say, "Caspian, get Bobo" he'll go looking around the house to find his toy.

> **TIP:** *"Teach your dog to round up your kids! Instead of going to get them yourself, you could combine this trick with "Speak" and tell your dog to "Go get Emma!" Once he finds her, he will bark once to let her know she's wanted.*

TEACHING TROUBLE

He's not getting it!

Don't tire your dog out. Five minutes at a time for a puppy and 7-10 minutes for an adult dog is a long training session. After that amount of time, their focus blurs. Even if your dog understands what you're trying to get him to do, he'll have a harder time remembering it later if he's tired.

15

Ring The Bell

Teach Your Dog To Ring A Jingle-bell When He Needs To Go Outside

Difficulty ·· Moderate
Prerequisite ·· Touch
Items Needed ························· Clicker, Treats, Jingle-bell

It's ten-thirty in the morning. You have to be at your friend's house at eleven, but you can't your dog's mess unattended in the dining room floor. You're a long time cleaning, scrubbing, and vacuuming. Eleven o'clock hits the mark and you haven't left yet. You jump in the car and onto the road full speed, and you still arrive twenty minutes late.

You apologize to your friend, explain to them in sparse detail why you came late. Later during a conversation unexciting, you hear their tiny dog's footsteps, then the tinkling and jingling of a bell. You ask them what it is. Oh it's my dog, they say, she's ringing the bell to tell me she has to go outside.

This is a useful trick, perfect as part of a house training routine for puppies. The attractiveness of using a bell to let you know when your dog needs to go out is that you can hear it ring all over the house. Using a bell, you'll be able to hear every single time your dog needs some time outside.

Step 1: Use a training stick to target the bell.

Step 2: When he touches the bell, click and treat.

Step 3: When he touches the bell on his own, click and jackpot.

Step 4: Whenever you take him outside, have him touch the bell first. The reward is to open the door.

Step 5: Your canine will, in a few days, learn that the door opens when he rings the bell.

> **TIP:** *"Keep the jingle bell on the door and well accessible to your dog. Also, make sure it is well tied to the string so it won't come off for your dog to swallow."*

OUR EXPERIENCE

Caspian was only a puppy when we taught him this trick. We taught him touch right away so that we could teach him to ring a bell to let us know that he needed to go outside. We threaded an old jingle bell left over from Christmas onto some twine, and wrapped it around our front door knob. We kept an eye on him before he quite learned to touch the bell, but it only took a couple of days for him to get the hang of it.

TEACHING TROUBLE

My dog rings the bell when he just wants to play.

You can eliminate this sly dog behavior by paying attention to certain times your dog usually goes out. If you have just taken your dog out and it isn't reasonable that he needs to go out again, or if your dog is in a particularly playful mood, don't open the door. You want the bell to be the signal for a quick "do your business" trip, not playtime.

16

Eliminate On Command

This Is Better Than Spending Hours Outside On A Cold Rainy Day

Difficulty ••••••••••••••••••••••••••••••••••••••	Easy
Prerequisite ••••••••••••••••••••••••••••••••••	None
Items Needed ••••••••••••••••••••••••••••	Clicker, Treats

Another practical command that should be taught is the "Park" (eliminate) command. I've spent many cold nights waiting on my dog. If you don't have a fenced in yard, and take your dog out on a leash, it can be pretty frustrating sometimes getting your dog to realize that he's there for a reason, and it's not checking out the neighborhood dog news.

Step 1: Designate a specific spot in your yard to make clean-up easier.

Step 2: Wait until he finishes eliminating, then click and treat.

Step 3: Do this each time, introducing a command such as "Park" or "Find a good spot."

Step 4: Be consistent, but vary the reward.

OUR EXPERIENCE

When it's cold and rainy outside, you can imagine how helpful an obedience command such as this would be. When teaching Caspian to "Park" on command, we would take a bag of treats and a clicker with us whenever we took him outside. As well as food treats, we would treat him in other ways as well, such as playing with a tennis ball or frisbee. If you start out by bringing your dog in immediately after he is finished, you may teach him to prolong parking so that he can explore more and have more time outside. Playing with Caspian afterwards trained him to do his business first, then playing and exploring comes afterwards.

> **TIP:** *"You don't have to give your dog a food treat each time you click. Try playing fetch with him for a while, or taking him on a nice, long walk! Dogs love attention just as much as they do food."*

TEACHING TROUBLE

After training for days, I say, "Park!" but he doesn't go!

Pay attention to Step 4: Be consistent, but vary the reward. Make sure you take something outside with you that your dog really wants, and make sure he knows you have it. If you've established that, then he'll try doing everything he can to get it, which will result in good behavior.

17

Teaching Leap

Here's How To Teach Your Dog To Leap Over A Hurdle

Difficulty •••••••••••••••••••••••••••••••••••••• Easy
Prerequisite •••••••••••••••••••••••••••••••••••• Come
Items Needed •••••••••••••• Clicker, Treats, Books, 2 Chairs, Stick

By this time, your dog should be progressing very nicely and has learned quite a few tricks! One impressive set of tricks involves leaping over or through objects. This is a staple for show dogs and makes quite a spectacle when you show dinner guests or friends. One word of caution: before attempting these jumping tricks, consult your veterinarian to see if jumping and leaping is right for your dog. It's not a good idea to teach jumping tricks to puppies, as it could damage their hips. And don't attempt this trick if your dog has a history of hip dysplasia.

Step 1: Have your dog "Sit" and "Stay" while you lay a stick on the ground. Cross over to the other side of the stick and call your dog. As soon as the dog crosses the stick, click and treat.

Step 2: Do this a few more times before adding height to the stick by placing a couple of thick books underneath it. Click and treat while he is crossing the stick.

Step 3: As your dog becomes accustomed to crossing the stick, add height with more books. Once it gets high enough that your dog has to jump over it, start saying "Leap" before clicking and treating. Keep doing this until your dog will leap when commanded!

OUR EXPERIENCE

Because I had already taught Caspian "Come," this trick was easy for him. I started out with my red stick laying on the ground. I said, "Caspian, come!" When he was crossing the stick, I clicked and treated. I crossed the stick and he followed me. Each time he crossed the stick, I would click and treat. Soon, I didn't have to call him - he knew he had to cross the stick in order to get his treat. I added some books to make the stick higher and waited for him to go across it. This time I said, "Leap!" and when he did, I

clicked and treated. Finally, I put the stick in the seats of the two chairs and told him to "Leap." He made a clear jump over the stick!

TEACHING TROUBLE

My dog keeps going around the stick instead of over it.

In some of the teaching sessions I had with Caspian, he wanted to come to me by going around the stick rather than jumping over it. This problem can be solved by ignoring his behavior until he crosses the stick. Another idea is to block off the remainder of your space so that he has no choice but to jump the stick to get to you.

He keeps knocking it over!

If your dog is knocking the stick over, that could be a sign that it is too high for him to jump. You want to make sure you don't injure your dog by having him leap too high. Lower it and try again. If you are sure that the height is reasonable, then you can click for the first couple times. But if he continues to knock it over, refrain from clicking/treating until he leaps without touching it. Then reward him well!

> **TIP:** *"Only go as high as is appropriate for your dog's breed and age. To avoid hip trouble later on, use moderation when teaching this trick and keep training sessions at around five minutes at a time."*

18

Jumping Through Hoops

Using The Leap Command, Teach Your Dog To Jump Through Hula Hoops

Difficulty •• Easy
Prerequisite •••••••••••••••••••••••••••••••••••••• Leap
Items Needed •••••••••••••••••••• Clicker, Treats, Hula-hoop, Helper

If you have ever been to the circus, you'll remember that act where the man comes out with his dogs and those big hula hoops. He holds the hoops high in the air and his dogs leap through and run around and leap through again, as fluently as a ballerina's grand jeté. Maybe you thought, "Wow, I wish I could get my dog to do that," but maybe you didn't know how, or if it was even possible, to train your dog to do that. Training your dog to leap through hoops is easy, and pretty soon, he'll be leaping through the air just like any professional circus dog.

Step 1: Let your dog get used to the hoop. Set it on the ground; click and treat when he approaches it.

Step 2: Have a helper hold the hoop (do not elevate the hoop) on the floor in front of him.

Step 3: Call your dog or lure him through the hoop with the touchstick. Click and treat as he walks through the hoop. Repeat this a few times so he will get used to walking through it.

Step 4: Hold the hoop a bit higher and tell him to "Leap!" Click and treat if he jumps through the hoop.

Step 5: Keep on giving the hoop more height, clicking and treating each time.

OUR EXPERIENCE

Caspian wasn't so sure about the hula hoop when we started out. Each time I got it out, he would slowly back up a step, then another, and finally leave the room. But I soon taught him that it wasn't anything to be afraid of. Now, jumping through hoops is one of his favorite things, and he rarely requires a treat to do it.

I sure did start out with treats, though! Each time he approached the hoop, which was lying motionless on the ground, I would click and treat. Then I had my helper hold the hoop upright as I guided Caspian through the hoop. He tried to go around it at first, but eventually he cooperated. Each time he went through the hoop, I clicked and gave him a treat. Soon, I thanked my helper and took the hula hoop, raising it a bit in the air. "Leap!" I told him. Since he already knew Leap, he jumped right through. I clicked and treated. Each time we did it again, I raised the hula hoop just a bit higher. Soon, he was jumping through them at a very decent height! As we practiced this trick more and more, we started using smaller and smaller hoops.

TEACHING TROUBLE

He hits the hoop every time!

It is OK to click and treat if your dog hits the hoop starting out. But soon you will want to eliminate this unwanted behavior by not clicking when any part of him touches the hoop. He will soon learn that he has to clear the hoop before he gets his treat.

TIP: *"Try using hoops of various sizes. Start out with a standard size hula hoop, but as your dog perfects the trick, try decreasing the size of the hoops. It's quite a spectacle to watch a full grown dog leap through a tiny hoop!"*

19

Jumping Over People

This Is A Great Backyard Circus Trick

Difficulty •••••••••••••••••••••••••••••••••••• Moderate
Prerequisite •••••••••••••••••••••••••••••••••• Leap
Items Needed ••••••••••••••••••• Clicker, Treats, Helper, Stick

Now that your dog can jump over sticks and through hoops, let's give him a bigger challenge. Get down on all fours and have your dog jump over your back. This is not only fun for your dog, but for the whole family. Involving people adds a lot of excitement to a simple jumping trick, and children think it is funny to see people get on their hands and knees so a dog can jump over them. This is a great trick for social events and is a staple for show dogs.

Step 1: If your dog can comfortably jump over a stick elevated about 25 inches from the ground then you can begin to teach him to jump over people who are on their hands and knees in the crawl position.

Step 2: Have your dog jump over the stick. Click & treat. (Repeat a few times).

Step 3: Have a helper kneel on their hands and knees.

Step 4: Hold the stick just over him. Have your dog jump over the stick. Click and jackpot. (If your dog won't jump over the stick with the person under it, try having the person lie down on the ground).

Step 5: After a few repetitions have your dog jump without using the stick. Click and treat.

Step 6: Try adding people spaced about 10 feet apart for a nice show at your next barbecue.

OUR EXPERIENCE

Caspian was hesitant to jump over a person, and we had to work with him to help him overcome his doubt. Both Caspian and I knew that he could complete the jump, but the idea of a person being there instead of a hoop or a stick was foreign to him. We started out by placing the jumping stick on top of the person's back and saying "Leap." He wouldn't jump, so we had to start by laying on the floor first just to get him used to the idea of crossing the jump stick with a person there as well. Once he got this concept, he was good to go.

> **TIP:** *"People can be even more unpredictable than dogs. So be sure that each of your volunteers understand that they should keep quiet and not move or stand up while the trick is in progress. Another great idea for this trick is to get dogs to jump over each other!"*

TEACHING TROUBLE

He won't jump over me!

Although it was easy to teach Caspian to jump over a stick, he would balk at jumping humans. Having the person lay down and lowering the stick helped. After Caspian got used to jumping with the volunteer flat on the floor, he was read to jump over the stick with the volunteer beneath it on hands and knees. Soon we didn't need to use the stick at all.

20

Go To A Place

Teach Your Dog To Go To A Previously Assigned Spot Or Marker

Difficulty •••••••••••••••••••••••••••••••••••• Moderate
Prerequisite •••••••••••••••••••••••••••••••••••• Touch
Items Needed ••• Clicker, Treats, Touchstick, Electrical Tape or Shiny Disk

"Go to a place" is a fundamental trick used in movie production. In this trick, you will teach your dog to go to a certain place, marked by a small piece of tape or shiny disk. You can also use this trick to teach your dog to lie down on his bed or sit on a rug. It can also be paired with other tricks for a more exciting show. This is an easy trick to teach and can be funny watching your dog prance on top of his mark, eager for a treat! This trick has many uses, one of which is to get your dog to pose with you for family portraits.

Step 1: Have your dog touch the touchstick. Click and treat.

Step 2: Place a piece of tape or a disk on the floor. Use the touchstick to point to the marker, and click/treat when he is on that spot. Practice this several times until your dog knows to go to the marker to get his treat.

Step 3: Call the marker by its name (mark, spot, disk, etc.) just as he steps into it. Click and treat. Repeat until you can say the name of the marker and he'll go right to it! Now, you can place the marker anywhere in the room where you want your dog to sit or lie down.

OUR EXPERIENCE

This was an interesting trick to teach Caspian. We previously had taught him to sit on our foyer rug by catching the behavior with the clicker; then attributing the name "Rug" to the action. But training him to go sit or lay down on a marker is much better, since we can place the marker down anywhere we want him to be. We chose some electrical tape for our marker and made an "X" with two small strips. We didn't want Caspian thinking that he was supposed to pick up the marker.

TEACHING TROUBLE

My dog will understand "Go to a place" after one session, but later in the day he can't remember it at all and we have to start over again!

This is perfectly normal. Keep practicing the trick and your dog will eventually remember what to do. Try keeping practice sessions to five or ten minutes and give him a generous break afterwards. But don't let the break be too long - come back to reinforce it within the hour. Also, always end on a good note. Sometimes your dog might start to get frustrated even after doing the trick several times. When this happens, he is very close to getting it. It's important to keep going so that you can end positively and with a jackpot.

> **TIP:** *"For a funny routine, teach your dog to "Go to a corner" using this trick and combine it with Act Ashamed (Trick #40). "You should be ashamed of yourself!" You can tell your dog, "Go sit in the corner!"*

21

Teach Your Dog To Spin

Teach Your Dog To Spin Around In Circles

Difficulty ·· Easy
Prerequisite ··· Touch
Items Needed ·················· Clicker, Treats, Touchstick

It may not be a very useful trick, but having your dog spin in circles is very impressive. You can pair this trick with other moves such as jumping tricks to create a dance routine! If you want to get fancy, you can teach your dog to spin left or spin right by your hand signal. Start out big and point in the direction you want him to go, associating that with your specific command, "Spin Left," or "Spin Right." For each training session, use smaller hand signals for a perfected trick.

Step 1: Using your touch stick, guide your dog around in a circular motion. As he makes a full turn, click and treat.

Step 2: Keep doing this several times, eventually adding a hand signal (circular motion with index finger).

Step 3: Use the touchstick less. When your dog can spin without the touchstick, add your command.

Step 4: Practice until your dog can spin at your command!

OUR EXPERIENCE

It was easy to teach Caspian this trick. I just started by having him play around with the touchstick, getting him used to touching it while I clicked and treated. Then, I said "Touch" as I moved it around in a circular motion around his body. Caspian turned his head around to follow the touchstick and his whole body followed. As he made a whole turn, I clicked and treated. I did this again and again until he was used to the motion. I then started using a hand signal (moving my finger around in a circular motion) to help him out and used the touchstick less. When he was able to spin without the touchstick, I started giving his command, "Spin!" Each time he would spin at my command I would click and treat.

TEACHING TROUBLE

My dog has ADD!

All dogs do! Make sure your dog is well rested and your treats are good. Also, clear the room of any distractions such as televisions, toys, or children that might get in the way of an excellent training session.

> **TIP:** *"You can also teach this trick by using the clicker to catch your dog in the act of chasing his tail!"*

22

High Five, Shake Hands

People Love It When Puppies Give Them Their Paws To Shake

Difficulty ••	Easy
Prerequisite ••••••••••••••••••••••••••••••••••••	Sit
Items Needed •••••••••••••••••••••••••••••••	Clicker, Treats

If you have an especially cute puppy (and what puppy isn't cute?), visitors think that it is absolutely adorable to be introduced with a tiny paw-shake just as if to say, "Hi, nice to meet you! Why yes, it is okay for you to rub my belly now!"

Step 1: Have your dog sit in front of you.

Step 2: Touch his paw and wait for him to offer lifting his paw (however slight). Click and treat.

Step 3: Say the word "Paw" each time he lifts his paw. Click and treat.

Step 4: Say the word "Paw" and click and treat when he lifts his paw.

Step 5: Shape the trick by rewarding only higher lifts.

OUR EXPERIENCE

When Caspian learned "Paw," I started out by having him sit. I waited for him to lift his paw. As soon as he lifted it, I clicked and treated. I waited again, and clicked and treated when he lifted his paw. It was okay that he was only lifting it up a little bit. I wanted to capture the good behavior, however slight it was. After a few times repeating this, Caspian figured out that he got a treat whenever he lifted his paw. He started doing it more frequently, and I started saying the word "Paw" whenever he lifted it. Soon, when I gave him the command, he lifted it! In other training sessions I was able to shape the behavior so that he lifted his paw higher and eventually placed it in my hand.

TEACHING TROUBLE

He will lift his paw, but only a little bit! How can I get him to lift it higher?

Click and treat at the beginning, no matter how high he lifts his paw, to encourage good behavior. Then, get tougher! Start to only click and treat when your dog lifts his paw higher. Vary the reward; give him tastier rewards for higher lifts. He may get frustrated, but he'll get it soon enough.

> **TIP:** *"You can encourage him to lift his paw by tickling the hollow behind his paw."*

23

Teach Your Dog To Shake

Teach Your Dog To Shake When Given The Command

Difficulty ••••••••••••••••••••••••••••••••••• Moderate
Prerequisite ••••••••••••••••••••••••••••••••••• None
Items Needed •••••••••••••••••••••••••••••••• Clicker, Treats

A dog that shakes on command can be quite an impressive trick! The only problem: You have to catch your dog in the act of shaking first. This isn't a behavior that happens often: such as sitting, laying down or even barking. Nor is it one that you can introduce with a touchstick, such as spinning or playing dead. You have to catch your dog in the act of shaking, which can be tricky. First, you have to be observant! When does your dog shake? When he gets up from a nap? When he comes back inside? After he's had a bath? Notice these and pick the one that will be the easiest to teach. Usually the most effective training session is immediately after a bath, when your dog is wet and frisky.

Step 1: Catch this trick with the clicker. Click and treat after you give him a bath or after you go outside in the rain when he shakes the water off.

Step 2: If he offers the behavior again click and jackpot.

Step 3: Click and treat and give the command "Shake" whenever he shakes.

Step 4: Give the command—when he shakes, jackpot.

OUR EXPERIENCE

In teaching this trick to Caspian, we had some trouble catching him in the act of shaking. We tried rubbing him down really good—which almost worked. He shook when we messed up his fur, but it was more confusing for him than when we would catch the behavior naturally. What we started doing is clicking when he shook after getting out of the bathtub, or when he came inside on a rainy day. Once we were able to figure out what made him shake, it was a matter of repetition for Caspian to get it.

> **TIP:** *"Treat big the first few times so your dog will be motivated to find out why he's being rewarded!"*

TEACHING TROUBLE

The behavior doesn't happen often enough for my dog to get it!

There are a few tricks you can try to get your dog to shake. First, make sure he's wet. You could try getting a spray water bottle and spritzing some water all on his face. You can also try rubbing your dog back and forth vigorously. This usually causes dogs to shake. Your main problem is getting your dog to realize what he's doing. When the action happens naturally, the dog doesn't think about it much. You have to point it out to your dog, "Hey, good job shaking there. I want you to do it again."

24

Teach Your Dog To Jump

Get Your Dog Excited, And Teach Him To Jump

Difficulty ••	**Easy**
Prerequisite ••••••••••••••••••••••••••••••••••••••	**Touch**
Items Needed ••••••••••••••••••••••	**Clicker, Treats, Touchstick**

This trick teaches your dog to jump straight up in the air. It's not teaching him to jump 'over' an object, rather, it teaches him to jump in the air, with all four paws off the ground. This trick paves the way for teaching your dog to jump rope, (Trick #45). Again, as we've said in the beginning of this book: before attempting any jumping tricks, consult your veterinarian to see if these tricks are okay for your dog to do. Again, it's not a good idea to teach puppies jumping tricks—it's possible to hurt their developing hips. And if your dog has any history of hip dysplasia, these jumping tricks can hurt your dog. Teaching your dog to jump is both fun for you and your dog. Just make sure a vet give you the okay so that you don't hurt your pet. The point of teaching your dog this trick is to have fun, and this trick especially encourages your dog to be excited. You'll find yourself getting pretty excited as well!

Step 1: Hold your touchstick high in the air so that he has to jump up to touch it. As soon as his legs come off the ground, click and treat. If he's having trouble, start out with just having your dog touch the touchstick closer to the ground, then gradually get higher.

Step 2: Do this several times until he can jump up and touch it without hesitating. Start saying "Jump" when he jumps up to touch the stick.

Step 3: Keep doing this until he jumps at your command. Gradually stop using the touchstick and use your command instead. Click and treat whenever he does this.

> **TIP:** *"Short sessions are the key to this trick. Jumping up and down is hard on dogs' hips, especially larger dogs, so keep that in mind when you are training your dog."*

OUR EXPERIENCE

The secret to this trick was first of all to get Caspian excited! Once Caspian was all happy and excited, I grabbed my touchstick and started out by re-acquainting him with it. I gave him a couple of easy ones on the ground, then got higher. I placed the touchstick high enough in the air so that he had to jump (with all four paws off the ground) in order to touch it. As soon as all four paws came off the floor, I clicked and treated. After the first few, I started saying "Jump" as I clicked and treated. I used a hand signal to help him out and took away the touchstick. As I did my hand signal, I also gave the command "Jump!" He did it right away.

TEACHING TROUBLE

My dog will only put his front two paws off the ground!

This was the hardest thing for Caspian to learn. The main thing that helped him out was that he knew he needed to touch the stick first in order to get the treat. When I held the touch-stick high enough so that he had to jump to touch it, he learned that he got his treat when his back paws left the floor.

25

Teach Your Dog To Roll Over

Perhaps The Most Famous of Tricks

Difficulty ··················	Moderate
Prerequisite ··············	Down, Touch
Items Needed ·············	Clicker, Treats, Touchstick

Teaching your dog this trick is a must. Along with "Sit" and "Down," this is one of the most well-known dog tricks. In fact, if a visitor comes over and asks you, "Does your dog know any tricks?" then proceeds to find out for herself, chances are high that she'll ask, "Come on boy, roll over." Have you ever wondered how to get your dog to roll over? It's more difficult than many other tricks, but with patience and a lot of encouragement, your dog will be rolling over on command.

Step 1: Have your dog lie down.

Step 2: Lure him with the touchstick or with your treat to have him move over to one hip and on his side. Click and treat.

Step 3: Use the lure to get him to go over on his back. (This may take time for some dogs). Click and treat.

Step 4: Continue using the lure to get him to roll all the way over. Jackpot when he does this. (Some people have used gently sloping ground to make it easier for the dog to roll all the way over).

Step 5: When your dog is rolling over more readily, stop using the lure. Expect more before you click and treat, but praise and jackpot when he performs well.

Step 6: After he is rolling over smoothly, start giving him the verbal command "Roll over." A circular hand signal is also helpful. Always praise and intermittently click and treat when he performs well.

OUR EXPERIENCE

Caspian learned this trick quickly, but with some frustration. I started out having him lie down. I guided the touchstick gently from one side of his head to the other, pushing it back. I told him in a gentle voice to touch it. He moved his head around and as

he did so he moved onto his back, his paws coming upwards. I clicked and treated. The second time I did this I waited for him to come up some more before I clicked and treated. Soon, he rolled all the way over. "Good boy!" I said, and gave him a jackpot. After doing this several times, Caspian got the hang of rolling over. When he started doing it more smoothly I used my command "Roll over" as I clicked and treated. Soon, I stopped using the touchstick and Caspian was able to roll over at my command.

TEACHING TROUBLE

He stands up to touch the stick rather than roll over to do it!

This part of the training process depends on you. Be very gentle in your movements and commands. Move the touchstick around slowly as you say in a low voice, "...Roll...over..." If you are slow and steady in your voice and actions, your dog's actions will be less reckless, too!

TIP: *"Try having your dog roll over on the same side each time to keep things consistent."*

26

Teach Your Dog To Sit Pretty

Begging Is Easy For Some Breeds, But Others Have A Harder Time

Difficulty ••••••••••••••••••••••••••••••••••	Moderate
Prerequisite ••••••••••••••••••••••••••••••	Down, Touch
Items Needed ••••••••••••••••••••••••••••	Clicker, Treats

While it's generally not a good idea for your dog to be truly begging for scraps at the table, getting her to "Sit pretty"—act like she's begging—is a fun and comical trick to teach. This is also a good trick to build other tricks on. You can get your dog to act like she's praying, or to reach for the sky if you make a gun-hand-gesture. This is also a good exercise for your dog, and is great for strengthening her back legs. As with any exercise, moderation is key. Start out slow, and gradually build up to where your dog is comfortable.

Step 1: Get down on your dog's level with your dog sitting in front of you.

Step 2: Let your dog smell a treat and then slowly lift it up above her.

Step 3: When she lifts her paws off the ground click and treat.

Step 4: Each time her hindquarters are on the floor and her front paws are up, say "Sit pretty" and click/treat.

Step 5: Repeat four or five times each training session.

OUR EXPERIENCE

In the books, trainers say that this is one of the easiest tricks to teach your dog. Many dogs perform this trick naturally as soon as you lift a treat above their heads. Unfortunately, Caspian is not one of those lucky dogs. I had a hard time teaching him to sit pretty, but we persevered together, and finally we conquered it! Now, Caspian has no trouble with this trick and enjoys the performance.

> **TIP:** *"This is a great strength-training trick to teach your dog, because it builds up strength in your dog's hindquarters!"*

TEACHING TROUBLE

He isn't strong enough to sit pretty!

You can help support your dog at first by supporting her front paws so that she can gain strength. Only expect him to hold the position on her own for a second or two at first and gradually build up the endurance so that she can stay in position for several seconds.

27

Teach Your Dog To Speak

Teach Your Dog To Bark When Given The Command

Difficulty ••••••••••••••••••••••••••••••••••••••	Easy
Prerequisite ••••••••••••••••••••••••••••••••••	None
Items Needed ••••••••••••••••••••••••••••••	Clicker, Treats

Congratulations! You are halfway finished learning 52 tricks! To celebrate, here's an easy trick to teach your dog, one which is both useful and beneficial for learning more complex tricks later on, such as notifying you of visitors, learning to count (Trick #43), or growling. One great reason to teach your dog to bark on command is that by teaching him to bark, you may actually cure a barking problem. You can teach this trick in such a way so that your dog only barks when you give him the command—which can be extremely beneficial for those with problem dogs (not to mention less expensive and more humane than an anti-barking collar).

Step 1: Get your dog to bark. For example, if you know that your dog barks when the doorbell is rung, then ring the bell, and when he barks say "Speak" and click and treat.

Step 2: After repeating this several times, try giving him the command "Speak." If he obeys and barks, give him a jackpot.

OUR EXPERIENCE

We were really anxious to teach Caspian how to "Count" (Trick #43), so we delved right into this trick when he was just a puppy. In training him, we used things like knocking on the door or ringing the doorbell to make him bark, but we also caught the behavior when he barked naturally. Now, we usually have him sit first before giving him the speak command, just so that he is paying attention and ready to speak.

TEACHING TROUBLE

My dog never barks. How can I train him to speak?

If your dog doesn't bark very often, take extra time to figure out ways to teach your dog. Notice when your dog makes any growling noise, however slight. Click and treat for these small things and once your dog can make these little 'yips' on command, ask more of him by clicking and treating only when he growls louder. Become pickier by clicking and treating only when you are satisfied with the way it sounds.

> **TIP:** *"Use this trick to teach your dog to count!"*

28

Teach Your Dog To Hush

Teach A Command That Will Stop Your Dog From Barking

Difficulty	Moderate
Prerequisite	None
Items Needed	Clicker, Treats

Hush. It's an incredibly useful command that saves your ears and peace of mind. Depending on the breed, your dog may or may not be a barker. If he is territorial at all, you may be dealing with a lot of barking problems. Barking is good - it warns you of potential danger, but it can be very annoying if the dog is barking at every jogger that goes by. With this trick, teach him to be silent when you give the command.

Step 1: Focus your attention on your dog while he is barking. If he looks at you and stops barking, even for a second, click and treat.

Step 2: Repeat this several times, eventually adding the word "Hush" as you click and treat.

Step 3: After several training sessions while your dog is barking, give your dog the command and click and treat when he hushes. Repeat this until he has mastered the trick. Each time you repeat, go for longer durations of silence.

Step 4: You can now add a hand signal to help with this trick. Use it whenever you give the command, and he'll associate it with the trick.

> **TIP:** *You usually have to 'catch' this trick by waiting until your dog starts barking. But if you have noticed certain things that cause your dog to bark at, such as a ringing doorbell or a light shining on a wall, use that to help teach this trick."*

OUR EXPERIENCE

Caspian can be a worrier. He barks at every dog that walks down the street, as well as walkers and joggers, not to mention the mailman and the poor FedEx guy. We almost didn't get a package one time because Caspian was barking so loudly. Even though he has a deep bark, he's made entirely of fluff and would probably lick a burglar to death instead of attacking. However, the barking issue was a problem that we wanted to fix, and the "Hush" command has done its job.

TEACHING TROUBLE

When I stare at my dog to get her attention, she just ignores me and keeps on barking.

You may have to get her attention some other way. Clear your throat, say her name, or show her the treat. Reward small successes, use more desirable treats, and soon she will respond.

29

Teach Your Dog To Tug

Teach Your Dog To Not Only Tug On A Toy, But Also Give

Difficulty	Easy
Prerequisite	Take It
Items Needed	Clicker, Treats, Tug Toy

Here is a fun trick that both you and your dog will enjoy. Some breeds will naturally play tug with you or with other dogs. Maybe your dog already knows how to play tug. But learning to tug on command (and alternatively giving on command) is good to know. This trick is used in movie production all the time, and is a staple for stunt dogs. They learn to tug a certain piece of cloth or rope, which can be affixed to actors (Fido saves Billy by pulling him out of the way of a speeding train, etc.). The "Give" command is also useful apart from the tug game itself. If your dog collects your things, such as socks or slippers, tell him to "Give" instead of chasing him all over the house. But of course, playing tug is a great way to spend time with your dog and further builds the bond between human and dog.

Teaching Your Dog To Tug:

Step 1: Take a rope toy and offer it to the dog and say "Take it." Reward your dog with praise when he moves toward the rope toy.

Step 2: When your dog takes it, gently shake and tug the rope toy to get the dog to hold and pull against the tugs.

Step 3: Click and treat when your dog tugs back on the rope toy. Use "Tug" as your command. Keep repeating this until your dog will tug at it eagerly.

Teaching Your Dog To Give

Step 1: With your dog pulling firmly on the rope, say "Give" at the same time offering a treat. When he drops the rope toy, click and give him the treat.

Step 2: Reinforce this trick by repeating four or five times per session. Pay special attention to the "Give" command. This is important for your safety. Make sure that your dog will stop the game with the "Give" command.

Step 3: Play tug several times a day. Each time you play the game make sure you use the commands saying "Take it" when you your dog takes the rope and "Give" when you want him to release the rope.

> **TIP:** *"Use a special toy to teach this trick, and use it only while learning this trick and playing tug. This will keep your dog excited about this special toy, and you can use this instead of a food treat."*

OUR EXPERIENCE

Caspian was very eager to tug on a new rope toy. Since he is a lab-radoodle, he gets very excited about playing, whether it's with a ball, frisbee, or toy, so he began tugging on the rope toy naturally.

TEACHING TROUBLE

My dog is uninterested in this trick. How will I get him to start tugging at the toy?

It will help if the toy you use to teach this trick is one of your dog's favorite toys, a new toy, or one that you bring out only for this occasion. Your dog will be interested if you are excited, and play it with him like a game. You can also tease him with it a bit before you begin to get him excited.

30

Open And Close A Door

Teach Your Dog To Open And Close Household Doors

Difficulty ●●●●●●●●●●●●●●●●●●●●●●●●●●●●●●●●●●●●	Moderate
Prerequisite ●●●●●●●●●●●●●●●●●●●●●●●●●●●●●●●	Tug, Touch
Items Needed ●●●●●●●●●●●●●●●●●●●●●●●●●●●●●	Clicker, Treats

You have a smart dog! He's learning all sorts of new tricks. One trick that takes two separate steps to learn is opening and closing a door. Keep in mind that dogs can only open certain kinds of doors; it's practically impossible for a dog to twist a doorknob. The way dogs open doors is by pulling a cloth or rope attached to a latch. When he pulls the latch, the door swings open. You can use this trick to teach your dog to let himself out, but only teach this if you have a fenced-in yard. You can use this trick for a variety of other uses, such as opening and closing the refrigerator door (pair this with "Bring a drink," Trick #46), or opening and closing a mailbox (you can teach your dog to get the newspaper or deliver a letter).

OPEN

Step 1: Tie a bandana or cloth around your door. Tell him to "Tug" it. Wait until he tugs the door open, then click and treat.

Step 2: Keep doing this, eventually saying, "Open" whenever he tugs the door open. Click and treat every time.

Step 3: After your training session, he should be able to open the door at your command.

CLOSE

Step 1: Put your touchstick on the door.

Step 2: Each time he touches it and moves the door a little, click and treat.

Step 3: Start waiting until he has pushed the door closed. Click and treat.

Step 4: Do this until he will close the door each time. Click and treat generously when he does this!

Step 5: Start saying "Close" when he closes the door. After repeating the action several times, he should close the door at your command.

OUR EXPERIENCE

This command is taught to assistance dogs to help disabled persons in opening and closing doors. You can see how helpful this would be to someone wheelchair bound. For us, we don't have a specific reason such as this for Caspian to open and close doors, and since we don't have a fenced-in yard, we definitely didn't want him to be able to open the front door to let himself out. Nevertheless, we use this trick to open and close the refrigerator door, in conjunction with the "Bring a drink" command (Trick #46), which might be the perfect trick for when company comes over.

> **TIP:** *"Make sure you understand that while teaching your dog to open doors, he may use his newly learned trick to escape from home on a rather boring day."*

TEACHING TROUBLE

My dog is tugging and pushing, but can't open or close the door.

Do you have a small dog? Obviously, smaller dogs can't open or close heavy doors. If you want to teach your small dog this trick, give him a lightweight door such as a toy cabinet to open and close.

31

Teach Your Dog To Fetch

If Your Dog Has Mastered Tug And Bring It, Teaching Fetch Is Easy!

Difficulty •• Easy
Prerequisite •••••••••••••••••••••••••••• Take it, Bring it, Tug
Items Needed •••••••••••••••••••••••••• Clicker, Treats, Tug toy

If your dog has mastered the "Tug" game and the "Bring it" command, then teaching him to fetch will be easy. Fetch comes naturally to some dogs, and to others it is a moderately easy trick to teach. Once your dog learns "Fetch," he will enjoy doing it not only for treats, but simply because it's just a fun game. Follow the steps carefully with your dog, and soon you will have another fun game to play with him.

Step 1: Start by playing tug. Say the "Take it" command when you want your dog to pick up the rope toy, and then the "Give" when you want him to release the rope.

Step 2: Have your dog "Give" the rope, but then toss it a few feet away. Say, "Take it." Click and treat when he picks up the rope.

Step 3: Generally, your dog should be excited about playing the tug game, and will usually come back to play some more. If he doesn't, repeat step two, this time getting him to bring it to you with the "Come" command. Say "Give" and click and treat.

OUR EXPERIENCE

Since Caspian is part retriever, fetching came naturally to him. We would throw a tennis ball, and Caspian would be extremely excited—he knew that this was going to be a fun game. He would run down our hallway as fast as he could, and puppy-pounce on the ball. But then, he would get distracted, and not know what to do. He would chase after the ball fine, but he wouldn't always bring it back. We worked with him using the "Come" command, and by clicking/treating. It didn't take him long to bring the ball back every time. Now playing fetch is his absolute favorite thing to do!

> **TIP:** *"Practice fetching different objects and at greater distances. Be generous with praise and click and treat when he performs well."*

TEACHING TROUBLE

My dog has learned to fetch, but he always brings it back slowly.

Three things: The first thing is to use great rewards. Yummy snacks, great praising, a nice walk...all these 'treats' are good to reinforce the dog's behavior. The second thing is your enthusiasm. If you're not at all excited about the game, how do you expect your dog to be? Go all out, be silly. If your dog sees you enjoying it, chances are he will enjoy it, too. The third thing is time. The more you reinforce this trick, the more your dog will learn to appreciate it! Keep positive and practice it several times per day. After a while, he will learn to love fetch and look forward to playing.

32

Teach Your Dog To Back Up

Teach Your Dog To Walk Backwards

Difficulty •••••••••••••••••••••••••••••••••• Easy
Prerequisite •••••••••••••••••••••••••••••••• None
Items Needed •••••••••••••••••••••••••• Clicker, Treats

This is a very useful trick to teach your dog, and one that will condition him for more advanced tricks later on, such as incorporating it into a dance routine. Complex routines are built using the foundations of simple tricks like spin, leap, and back up. Think up creative ways to use "Back" with other tricks for a more impressive show.

Step 1: With your dog standing facing you, walk forward toward him. When he takes a step backwards, click and treat.

Step 2: Continue stepping forward. When he takes multiple steps backwards, click and treat.

Step 3: Practice this until he understands that if he backs up, he deserves a treat. Start walking toward him less. You can use a signal instead (Try waving the back of your hand toward him, or taking a single step forward).

Step 4: Once he has learned this, say "Back" as he backs up and as you give the hand signal. Do this several times until well learned. Remember to click and treat when he cooperates.

Step 5: Give him the command and see if he'll back up! Click and treat well each time he obeys. Reinforce with extra training sessions.

> **TIP:** *"A narrow hallway or a place where movement is restricted can help in teaching this trick."*

OUR EXPERIENCE

Teaching Caspian this trick was pretty straightforward. We would walk toward him, and click/treat when he would back up. Sometimes he would try to move out of our way instead of backing up, so we decided to relocate to our upstairs hallway—so the walls would constrict his movements. He soon got the idea, and we then attributed the command "Back up" along with the hand signal. We usually use the "Back up" command for him to back up and sit before tossing him a treat or toy.

TEACHING TROUBLE

My dog won't start backing up unless I advance toward him.

That's where the signal comes in. Try using the signal as you walk toward your dog each time. Then, gradually stop walking forward, but keep the hand signal. Be patient and give your dog time to think about it. Also, remember to take enough breaks and don't wear your dog out. Short sessions are the most successful!

33

Teach Your Dog To Yawn

This Trick, Like "Speak," Is Best Caught With The Clicker

Difficulty •••••••••••••••••••••••••••••••••••••• Moderate
Prerequisite •••••••••••••••••••••••••••••••••••••• None
Items Needed •••••••••••••••••••••••••••••• Clicker, Treats

The clock says the time is eleven-thirty. It's dark out and you're tired, and the couple on the couch haven't stopped talking. They are your friends, or used to be—you're not so sure now. But the greyhound in the corner is your friend. "Come here boy," you whisper under the jabbering of the couple. He lays down by your legs and you look at him. You stare into his eyes and say, "Are you tired?" He smacks his lips and yawns, his great teeth revealing themselves, then disappearing again. "Yes, I know you're tired," you say and pat his head. "I am too." Your friends get the message.

Step 1: Most dogs will yawn when they are anxious. You can use that to help you catch the yawn. Look for your dog to yawn when he wants to go outside or wants a ball or toy that you are holding. When he yawns, click and treat. Because this trick has to be 'caught' with the clicker, it can be fairly difficult, and you have to time your clicks just right.

Step 2: When he starts to offer a yawn because he has been treated for it, go ahead and give the command you want to associate with his action. It could be "Yawn," "Tired," or "Sleepy," but in any case, be consistent with your command. Repeat three to four times per session.

Step 3: After several sessions of training your dog to yawn, give him the command and see if he will respond with a yawn.

OUR EXPERIENCE

Because we have to catch Caspian in the act of yawning, it can be frustrating when trying to get him to yawn multiple times in a training session. Caspian will lick his muzzle and yawn if he is anxious, so sometimes during our training session, we would turn around and not say anything for a few seconds. Caspian, not knowing what to do, would then get a little anxious. An assistant would either click or let the trainer know when to click if he yawned (you won't be able to see your dog if your back is turned). This trick was more frustrating for Caspian in general. He knew that he was being clicked and treated for something that had to do with his mouth, but didn't quite understand at first.

If your dog gets frustrated during a training session, cut back on the amount of time for each session, but always try to end on a high note.

TEACHING TROUBLE

My dog doesn't understand that he's being clicked for yawning. How can I fix this problem?

Since a yawn is a natural response that a dog might give for either being tired or anxious, he usually doesn't even notice when he's doing it. Making him aware that he is yawning is the key to this trick. It may take several training sessions, but eventually your dog will get it!

> **TIP:** *"This trick presents better if you use a cute command like "Are you sleepy?" or "It's bedtime."*

34

Bringing Your Slippers

Teach Your Dog To Bring You Your Slippers, Or Any Other Object

Difficulty ••••••••••••••••••••••••••••••••••• Moderate
Prerequisite •••••••••••••••••• Learn Names, Take it, Bring it
Items Needed ••••••••••••••••••••••••••••••••• Clicker, Treats

This trick is a combination of "Take it," "Bring it," and "Give" (See "Tug," Trick #29). When you tell your dog to get your slippers, he will take them, bring them, and drop them right at your feet. What if you lost your slippers? Wouldn't this be a helpful trick! Just tell your dog "Get my slippers!" and off he'd go. In no time he would come back with the slippers and drop them by your feet. Some dogs can bring both slippers at the same time. But if you're having difficulty getting your dog to bring both slippers, keep your slippers together with a couple small pieces of Velcro tape. You don't have to keep them together, however. Your dog will do just as fine getting them one at a time.

Step 1: Using the "Learn Names" trick, teach your dog the name of whichever object you want him to bring you. For this particular trick, we want him to learn the name, "Slippers."

Step 2: Now that he knows what the name of the object is, tell him to "Get my slippers." Click and treat.

Step 3: Tell your dog to "Take it" and "Bring it." If he does so, click and treat.

Step 4: Now, try combining all three tricks. First, say, "Get my slippers!" Then, "Take it," "Bring it," and "Give." If he does what you ask, click and give him a generous treat. Repeat this until you have a polished trick.

> **TIP:** *"When shaping this trick, have your dog take the top part, or toe of the slippers each time so that they're not soggy when you put them on!"*

OUR EXPERIENCE

This was one of our favorite tricks to teach Caspian, and one of his favorites too. He does really well at learning names of things—he knows his toys by each of their names. So we introduced the slippers in the same kind of way. Because he was really excited about this trick, the slippers themselves were the reward. We realized, however, that he thought of the slippers as a toy, and would get preoccupied and play with them when we asked him to retrieve them for us. He would eventually bring them, but he would want to play with them first. To fix this problem, we clicked/treated only when he brought them back faster. We then conditioned him to bring them as soon as we asked for them.

TEACHING TROUBLE

My dog can do each of the initial tricks ("Take it," "Bring it," and "Give"), but is having trouble blending them all together. What do I do?

Repetition is the key to this trick. As you practice it more, it will flow together better and you won't have to use each command to get him to do what you want him to do. Eventually, you will have him learn that the command "Get my slippers" means to take the slippers, bring them, and drop them at your feet!

35

Bringing The Leash

Teach Your Dog To Bring You His Leash

Difficulty •• Easy
Prerequisite •••••••••••••••••••••• Take it, Bring it, Learn Names
Items Needed •••••••••••••••••••••••••••••• Clicker, Treats, Leash

Like "Bring Slippers," this trick builds off of the "Learn Names" trick. In this trick, you will teach your dog to bring you his leash when you are ready to take him outside for a walk. This is quite an impressive trick, and makes your dog appear super smart. My grandmother came for a visit one day, and I nonchalantly asked Caspian for his leash to take him outside. When he came trotting back with the leash dangling from his mouth, my grandmother laughed and pronounced him "the smartest dog." I'm sure your guests will do the same!

Step 1: Set the leash on the floor. Tell him to take it. Click and treat when he does.

Step 2: Go to the door. Tell him to take the leash, bring it, and drop it in your hands. Click and treat.

Step 3: Repeat the take it, bring it, drop it action several times, saying, "Leash!" when he drops it in your hands.

Step 4: Eliminate the "Take it, "Bring it," and "Give" commands and start only using "Leash." You can also use a hand signal to give him a hint.

Step 5: Command him to get his leash. Click and Jackpot if he obeys you, and take him outside for a long walk!

OUR EXPERIENCE

Although this trick took several training sessions to teach, "Leash" was a moderately easy trick for Caspian to learn. I started out with the leash on the floor. "Take it!" I said. He did, and I clicked and treated. The next time, I said "Take it," "Bring it," and "Give." Each time he did this for me I would click and treat, saying "Leash!" Many times, when he would successfully drop it into my hands, I would take him outside as a reward instead of a treat. Soon, Caspian was able to bring me his leash whenever I gave him the command. Whenever we go outside, he brings it to me every time!

> **TIP:** *"Put the leash somewhere so your dog has easy access to it, such as draped over a closet knob or in a basket near the door."*

TEACHING TROUBLE

He won't drop it in my hands!

If he has learned "Take it," "Bring it," and "Give," then you can be picky. If he doesn't put it in your hands, he doesn't get a walk, or a treat either. If he successfully brings it to you and drops it on the floor, tell him to take it again and drop it in your hands. Immediately click and reward when he does drop it into your hands.

36

Bringing The Dish

Teach Your Dog To Bring You His Dish When He Is Hungry

Difficulty •• Easy
Prerequisite •••••••••••••••••••••••• Learn Names, Take it, Bring it
Items Needed ••••••••••••••••••••••••• Clicker, Treats, Food Dish

Another useful trick. When your dog brings you his dish, not only does it make him look smart but it saves you the effort of having to get it. How does your dog tell you he's hungry? Pawing at his dish, knocking it over, barking? Here's a simple and cute way for your dog to let you know that he needs to be fed.

Step 1: Use the "Learn the Names of Everything" to teach him to touch his dish on command.

Step 2: Teach him to hold the dish in his mouth using the "Take it" command. Your dog may not like holding a metal dish in his mouth, but this trick is worth the extra effort. Take extra time with this step.

Step 3: With the dish on the floor say the name "Dish." When he starts to touch the dish say "Take it." If he takes the dish in his mouth at all click and treat.

Step 4: With your dog holding the dish in his mouth say "Bring it." Click and treat when he takes a few steps toward you with the dish.

Step 5: As you repeat these steps, introduce the command "Get your dish." When he takes it, click and treat

Step 6: Give the command "Get your dish." Click and treat when he brings it to you. Gradually extend the distance from the bowl as you perfect this trick.

> **TIP:** *"After several training sessions, your dog may naturally bring his dish to you to tell you he's hungry!"*

OUR EXPERIENCE

Teaching "Dish" wasn't too hard once I taught Caspian to learn its name. I first had him touch the dish, eventually teaching him that its name was "Dish." The next step was getting him to pick it up. This was more difficult because his dish is heavier than other objects we have trained with before. I clicked and treated for small advances towards the behavior I wanted. Eventually, he was able to carry it completely in his mouth. I then told him to "Bring it." Since he knew these commands already, it wasn't very hard to string them together into this nice trick — "Get Your Dish."

TEACHING TROUBLE

What if my dog's dish is too heavy for him?

Your dog will most likely be able to carry it. It could be that he's just not used to carrying something that bulky and heavy. It's a good idea to start out small and click and treat for small advances toward the dish. You could even build up to this trick by having him learn to take lighter things in his mouth, then gradually teaching heavier things until he is able to hold the dish. Of course, if you have a small dog, a metal dish might be too bulky for him to pick up. You can try using a smaller dish. Another idea is to teach "Fetch a Drink" first to get him gradually used to carrying heavier things in his mouth by filling up the drink bottle a little at a time.

37

Put Toys Away

Get Your Dog To Gather Up All His Toys Into A Basket

Difficulty •••••••••••••••••••••••••••••••••••••• Hard
Prerequisite •••••••••••••••••• Learn Names, Take it, Bring it
Items Needed •••••••••••••••••• Clicker, Treats, Basket, Dog Toys

So you've finally taught your kids to put their toys away—but what about your dog? This trick is helpful, and also impressive. Give your dog a simple command and watch him go around the house and gather up all his dog toys together and drop them in a basket or box.

Step 1: Get a large box or basket. Gather all your dog's toys and put them in a pile.

Step 2: Give the command, "Put toys away" then point to each toy and say, "Take it," then "Bring it" and "Drop it" into the basket. When he does this, click and give him a treat.

Step 3: Do this several more times. After several training sessions, you should be able to just say, "Put toys away" and he will put them all in. Give him a big treat each time.

Step 4: Next put each toy farther away from the basket. Work with him to find all his toys and put them away into the basket when you give the command.

> **TIP:** *"Sometimes you'll feel like treating him for his good efforts, but only click and treat when your dog actually drops the toy into the basket. If it's only halfway in it counts, but it doesn't count if it's not in at all."*

OUR EXPERIENCE

It was difficult to teach Caspian to put his toys away, but since he already knew to "Take it," "Bring it" and "Drop it," that was a big help! I spread an assortment of toys across the floor with a big basket in the middle. I told him to take one of his toys, to bring it and drop it in the basket. He wouldn't drop it in the basket at first, but I would go ahead and click for the effort. Eventually I became stricter in what I was looking for, and only clicked when he actually got the toy in the basket. As soon as all his toys were in the basket he got a big treat! I would always say "Put toys away" whenever he would put any toy—or all toys—in the basket. We did several sessions of this until he was able to put them all in the basket when I gave him the command: "Caspian! Put toys away!"

TEACHING TROUBLE

He won't put them all in!

Probably the hardest thing I had to work with for Caspian was grouping all his toys together in one command. Sometimes by the time they get all their toys in, they forget what they did at the beginning. One thing you can do is start out with only three toys. When your dog puts them in, click and treat. Do this several times, then add another toy. When he puts all four in, click and treat.

38

Teach Your Dog Find It

This Is Both A Fun And Useful Game To Play With Your Dog

Difficulty •••••••••••••••••••••••••••••••••••••• Moderate
Prerequisite •••••••••••••••••••••••••• Learn Names, Sit, Stay
Items Needed •••••••••••••••••••••••••••• Clicker, Treats, Dog Toy

This trick can be taught with any toy or item and could turn out to be very useful if you lose something. Besides the practical usefulness of this trick, this is a really fun game to play with your dog! Have your dog go out of the room and sit, then hide the object somewhere in the next room. The object could be anything: one of his toys, an article of clothing, but make sure he knows what he's searching for. For a more advanced performance, hide something with a less noticeable scent, such as the TV remote or a set of keys.

Step 1: Have your dog sit.

Step 2: Hold up an object that he is familiar with (he knows its name) and let him smell it.

Step 3: Place the object under something obvious (like a towel), and say "Find it." You might add the name of the object if he doesn't find it quickly ("Find it" Bunny). Click and treat when he touches the object.

Step 4: Repeat several times, but each time you repeat move the object to a different location, getting progressively more difficult. Start having your dog sit and wait in an adjacent room. Click and treat each time.

Step 5: Let him smell and then hide other objects that he is not familiar with and give the "Find it" command.

> **TIP:** *"Use the same terms each time! In other words, don't tell your dog to "Find it," while still using "Get it," "Where is it?" and "Search" intermittently. Consistency is the key!"*

OUR EXPERIENCE

When I first taught this trick, I was using an old Atlanta Braves hat that I used to wear. Because the hat had a lot of my smell on it, it was really easy for Caspian to pick up on. It started out basically by accident. I hadn't planned on teaching him this trick. I was just playing around with the old hat, playing keep away, putting it underneath things for him to dig it out. I had him go out of the room, and I stuck it partially underneath the rug, then called him. He sniffed around a few seconds before finding it. Although I had stumbled upon this trick by accident, I got my clicker and started rewarding him for finding the hat. Because he had learned the term "Find it," in relation to finding things with my scent on it, when I lost a set of car keys in the backyard one day, I told Caspian to "Find it." Although he didn't know what he was looking for, he went to the thing that had our scent on it. In just a few minutes, he had found my keys.

TEACHING TROUBLE

My dog doesn't understand what I want him to do.

Some dogs have great noses, others don't. But your dog doesn't have to be a bloodhound to learn this trick. When starting out, make sure the toy you use to hide is one he really likes. Also make sure he knows its name. Start out easy; you may not want to even hide it starting out. Put it in plain sight and encourage your dog to touch it. After that, then you can start to hide the toy in progressively more difficult spaces.

39

Teach Your Dog To Catch

This Is Both A Fun And Useful Game To Play With Your Dog

Difficulty •• Easy
Prerequisite •• Sit
Items Needed •••••••••••• Clicker, Treats, Tennis Ball or Plush Toy

Dogs have many abilities that humans aren't capable of. Their ears can pick up sounds well past the range that you or I could hear. They have a nose that can smell a thousand times better than humans. And, while nearsighted, they can sense movement and motion 10-20 times better than their owners, making them ideal for catching things out of the air. Add this to their speed, and you have a powerful treat-snatching-machine. Dogs may not catch naturally, but they can learn in just a few training sessions. Pretty soon, your dog could be making spectacular airborne catches!

Step 1: Start out with a short distance and a good treat. Throw the treat to your dog. If he doesn't catch it, take the treat away and try again. If he does catch it, click and treat, offering lots of praise.

Step 2: Keep doing this until he is catching well. Start saying "Catch" while he is catching them.

Step 3: Give him the command "Catch!" and throw the treat. Give him lots of praise if he catches it at your command!

Step 4: Use other objects like tennis balls or plush toys to give him more experience with catching. Just make sure that you aren't tossing him something too small that could be a choking hazard. The more he practices, the better he will get!

> **TIP:** *"Practice makes perfect. Don't despair if your dog doesn't catch well at first. Reward good behavior even if he tries to catch it and misses. Give him praise and encourage him to keep on trying!"*

OUR EXPERIENCE

Since "Fetch" is Caspian's favorite game, we use it every day for exercise. For a little variety, we started sending him out before we threw the ball. Because he had learned catch, he started catching the tennis ball while it was still in the air. He often makes some very spectacular catches. Make sure that you use a very soft ball if you try this with your dog. Also, if you notice that your dog is jumping to catch food treats and toys, check with your vet to see if jumping is good for your dog. You want to make sure your dog is in good health before attempting any jumping tricks.

TEACHING TROUBLE

He's not catching anything!

Some dogs are spectacular catchers, others are not. It's an instinct that all dogs have, but some breeds more than others. Just be patient—it may take a bit longer for your dog to learn this trick.

40

Act Ashamed

Teach Your Dog To Act Ashamed If One of His Other Tricks Goes Awry

Difficulty •••••••••••••••••••••••••••••••••••••• Moderate
Prerequisite •••••••••••••••••••••••••••••••••••••• None
Items Needed •••••••••••••••••••••••• Clicker, Treats, Scotch Tape

Just as a comedian needs a handful of one-liners when his joke doesn't go over too well, it's good to have a trick to fall back on if your dog doesn't quite perform up to the level you were expecting.

Let's say you have some dinner guests over, and you want to show off that new trick you taught Bella yesterday. You had taught her "Get Slippers," (Trick #34) and you're excited to show your friends how smart your dog is. Well, after telling her to retrieve your slippers, she's gone for a long time... After calling her, she comes slinking back and drops the remnants of a thoroughly chewed slipper at your feet. Your dinner guests are trying their best not to laugh, they know you're embarrassed. Well, one trick that you did drill over and over is this one. "Bella! You should be ashamed of yourself!" Bella whines and lays down, puts her paw over her head. Your audience bursts into surprised laughter.

Step 1: Put some Scotch tape or a sticky note on your dog's nose so that she paws at it. Click and treat.

Step 2: Repeat this a few times, but add in your command. Use the word "Ashamed" as a command—later you can use it in a phrase like, "You should be ashamed," or "Aren't you ashamed?" Use this command each time she paws at her nose.

Step 3: Take the tape off and give your command. Give her a jackpot if she paws at her nose!

Step 4: If you wish, you can accompany this trick with her lying down. While teaching her, have her lie down before she paws at her nose.

> **TIP:** *"A good hand signal would be putting your hands on your hips!"*

OUR EXPERIENCE

This trick was so much fun to teach Caspian. I started with some Scotch tape and put it on his nose. Since Caspian didn't want the tape on his nose, he naturally started pawing at it. Immediately I clicked and treated. Each time he did it, I would click and treat, saying "Ashamed." After several times practicing with the tape, I gave him the command and he would paw at his nose. Soon, I was able to take the tape off his nose and give him the command again. He did it!

TEACHING TROUBLE

My dog won't rub his nose without the tape!

Try cuing the behavior by gently scratching her nose with your finger. That should trigger a memory and she'll obey you. You can use this hint less and less to perfect the trick.

41

Left And Right

Teach Your Dog To Walk Next To Your Left And Right Sides

Difficulty ••••••••••••••••••••••••••••••••••••••	Moderate
Prerequisite ••••••••••••••••••••••••••••••••••••	Touch
Items Needed ••••••••••••••••••••	Clicker, Treats, Touchstick

Does your dog know his left and right? This is an easy trick to teach. When you take him out on a leash, does he tangle it around your legs? It may be useful to tell him "Left" or "Right" and keep yourself untangled from the leash. Not only is this a good trick to show off your smart dog, this is a useful command that professionally trained assistance dogs are expected to learn.

Step 1: With your touchstick, have your dog go around your right side and stand by your left side. Click and treat.

Step 2: Keep doing this, eventually saying, "Left" as soon as he stands by your left side.

Step 3: Repeat this action until he no longer needs the touchstick and can go to your left side at your command.

Step 4: Do the same thing, this time teaching him to go from your left side to your right side.

OUR EXPERIENCE

When teaching Caspian "Left" and "Right," I began by using the touchstick. I would motion him to both sides, and clicking/treating. However, he easily became confused, and didn't quite get what he was being clicked for. Sometimes there are more than one way to teach a trick. So I had him first sit, then I turned around and patted my leg as to which side I wanted him to go to. When I motioned with my hand, he would come to that side. As he did so, I would say the command either "Right" or "Left." I then started just saying the command, and leaving out the hand motion, and only clicking/treating for a correct performance. I

would mix up the commands, just to see if he really knew the difference between "Right" and "Left." Using the touchstick is a great way to teach this trick, but you may feel the need to tweak the steps a little to suit your own needs.

TEACHING TROUBLE

My dog is getting his left confused with his right! What do I do?

Try treating "Left" and "Right" as two separate tricks if this is happening. Usually, you want to teach both "Left" and "Right" so that your dog can differentiate between the two, but if he is getting easily confused, start with one, then move to the other. Try focusing on just one of them per training session. Hand cues are also important here. If your dog is paying attention and wants to find out what you're asking him to do, he'll look for hand signals, motions, or a direction from you to point him where he needs to go.

> **TIP:** *"You can gradually stop using the touchstick by guiding your dog with big hand motions. Then, you can make your hand motions smaller for a polished performance!"*

42

Teach Your Dog Weave

Your Dog Can Weave Just Like Professionaly Trained Agility Dogs!

Difficulty •• Hard
Prerequisite ••• Touch
Items Needed ••• Clicker, Treats, Touchstick, Cones, Buckets, or Solo Cups

When you watch dog agility competitions, one of the most spectacular sections has to be the weave poles. These championship dogs have trained hard and long to weave back and forth in between the poles at break-neck speed. Trainers say this is one of the hardest sections of agility competitions. Although there is difficulty involved, most dogs end up loving the weave poles. So even if you aren't trying to enter an agility competition, you can teach your dog this fun and exciting trick, using basic household products, and of course your clicker.

Step 1: Set up obstacles, such as small orange cones (bought at Wal-mart), buckets, or even red plastic cups in a straight line. Start with three or four, and space them 24-30 inches apart. With your touchstick, guide your dog in and out of the obstacles, starting from the left side. When he goes in and out of one or two, click and treat. Continue to do this until he goes in and out of all of them.

Step 2: After getting your dog used to these motions, start saying "Weave" when he is finishing up his trick. Click and treat.

Step 3: Do this several times until your dog will weave at your command. This is a hard trick to teach, and it may take many training sessions. Fully expect your dog to go after the obstacles and try and play with them. Gently guide his attention back to your treats, and get him focused again on the touchstick.

OUR EXPERIENCE

Using the touchstick, I guided Caspian through each obstacle. At first, I clicked and treated as he went through two or three obstacles. Then, I would click and treat as he wove through each one. At the end, I would say "Weave!" and click and treat. We did this several times until Caspian could weave in a flowing tempo. Soon, I was able to use less touchstick and let him do it on his own.

> **TIP:** *"Encourage your dog to weave faster and faster! Make him excited by being excited yourself. Give him bigger treats if he goes at a fluent tempo."*

TEACHING TROUBLE

He does it with the touchstick fine - but he won't do it on his own!

If you think you have used the touchstick long enough and would like to have him do it on his own, but he's not responding, try using your finger to guide him. That will help him know what to do, and you can gradually get rid of the hinting.

43

Teach Your Dog To Count

Teach Your Dog To Count And Solve Simple Math Problems

Difficulty •••••••••••••••••••••••••••••••••• Moderate
Prerequisite •••••••••••••••••••••••••••••••••• Speak
Items Needed •••••••••••••••••••••••••••••• Clicker, Treats

Here is a fun and impressive trick that proves that your dog is as smart as Einstein (mmm ... or at least as smart as Einstein's dog). The trick is to get your dog to bark until a subtle cue causes him to stop. Then you can have him bark out any number of barks to answer various mathematical questions. This trick is not that hard to teach, but it does take patience and longer periods of time than most tricks in order to shape the behavior correctly. It is really worth the effort because it shows that your dog really counts for something.

Step 1: Have your dog sit facing you.

Step 2: Hold a treat in your left hand and hold your right hand up. (Here we are getting the dog to associate the speak command with the visual command of holding your right hand up). Also look your dog in the eye (I look directly into his right eye).

Step 3: Have the dog speak, and treat when he barks.

Step 4: Repeat. But this time only drop your hand (also avert your eyes) and treat when he barks twice. (This may take some patience).

Step 5: Work on this several times a day until your little Einstein realizes he must continue to bark until you drop your hand.

Step 6: Gradually fade from holding your right hand up so that your dog will use your eyes as the cue to stop speaking.

Step 7: Keep refining this trick until he has a smooth flow of barks and stops as soon as you avert your eyes.

> **TIP:** *"Have your guests think of simple math problems for your dog to answer, but make sure you do the math right!"*

OUR EXPERIENCE

While teaching our dog to count, we started by re-familiarizing him with the speak command. While doing this, we introduced a small cue: looking down and staring at him directly into his right eye. When getting him to speak, we began with clicking right after he barked once, then once he was progressing well, we started clicking after multiple barks. Each time we wanted him to stop barking, we would immediately break our eye contact, and click and treat. Once this was accomplished, we could cue him to start barking by rotating our head down and looking at his right eye. Once he finished barking, we would break our eye contact, and reward him for a job well done. This is how Caspian can solve math problems given by friends - we keep him barking using this subtle cue. We just have to make sure we do the math right ourselves.

TEACHING TROUBLE

My dog doesn't always stop barking on time!

Keep working with him. If you click as soon as you avert your eyes, he will likely stop barking. If your dog (or you) makes a mistake during a performance, put your hands on your hips and say, "Oh! Einstein, I'm ashamed of you," which cues his "Act Ashamed" trick (Trick #40) for a good laugh.

44

Teach Your Dog To Bow

At The End Of A Performance, Take A Bow With Your Dog!

Difficulty •• Easy
Prerequisite ••••••••••••••••••••••••••••••••••••••• None
Items Needed •••••••••••••••••••••••••••••••• Clicker, Treats

By now your dog most likely knows a whole repertoire of tricks, from simple ones such as "Sit," to more complicated ones like "Put Toys Away." With good treats, your dog can perform a string of impressive tricks for your friends—but you are still lacking one thing: an ending. The perfect way for your dog to end a performance is the same way any professional does: with a bow. If you follow these three simple steps, you will be set up for a perfect dog show.

Catch The Behavior

Step 1: Dogs naturally bend forward and put their head near the ground to invite play. Start 'rough-housing' with your dog. Whenever he starts to get into the "bow" position, click and treat. Keep doing this until he starts doing it on his own.

Step 2: Start saying "Bow" whenever he gets into the Bow position; then click and treat.

Step 3: Keep doing this until he will bow at your command! Always give your dog a jackpot when he obeys your command for the first time.

OUR EXPERIENCE

My dog loves to play. Whenever I would play with him, and start to chase him, I noticed that he would "Bow" by laying his front two legs down before he ran from me. I decided to shape this behavior into a "Take a bow" trick. I started by chasing him. As soon as he bent forward with his front legs, I clicked and treated. We did this again and again until he understood that I was clicking for his "Bow" position. Soon, he started to do it more fre-

quently. I used the command "Bow" whenever I clicked. Eventually, Caspian was able to obey my command when I told him to bow. And it all started by playing a game of chase!

TEACHING TROUBLE

My dog never bows when he is playful!

When does he bow? Is it when he gets up from his nap to stretch? Or when he is meeting other dogs? Notice when he gets in that position and use that to shape the behavior.

> **TIP:** *"Although many trainers teach "Bow" by forcing the dog into a bow position, we believe it is much easier and less frustrating to capture the natural behavior of your dog.*

45

Jumping Rope

Teach Your Dog To Jump Rope, A Difficult But Funny Routine

Difficulty •• Hard
Prerequisite •••••••••••••••••••••••••••••••••••••• Jump
Items Needed •••••• Clicker, Treats, Light-weight Jump Rope, Table

This is a fun trick to teach your dog, and good exercise for him as well. Since this is a difficult trick, read the steps carefully and be patient with your dog. Soon he will be jumping rope, and loving it! If your dog is still young, you might want to wait before teaching him to jump rope: jumping too much may be hard on his hips. Before any jumping trick, always first check with your vet to see if your dog can handle it.

Step 1: Put your dog on a low table. Ask him to jump. Click and treat. Your dog should stay in the same place so he won't fall off the table.

Step 2: Tie the jump rope to another object. Let your dog get used to the jump rope by moving it back and forth.

Step 3: Give the jump rope almost a full turn, stopping before it crosses your dogs legs. At this point, tell him to "Jump." When he does, slide the jump rope underneath. Do this several times, clicking and treating.

Step 4: As your dog gets more accustomed to the jump rope, you will be able to have smoother rotations. Work with your dog until he can do it just right.

OUR EXPERIENCE

It took extra patience to teach Caspian "Jump rope" (and more than a few handfuls of treats), but hard work pays off. At first Caspian was distracted with the jump rope, and he would get frustrated after long sessions, but as we practiced more and more he stopped thinking about the rope and started focusing on jumping. Once he did this, it became easier for us to work the rope, and soon the trick was working smoothly. Since Caspian's accident we haven't worked with this trick since jumping up and down stresses his back hip. If you have a larger dog breed or if your dog has any history of hip dysplasia, consult your veterinarian before attempting this trick.

TEACHING TROUBLE

My dog is scared of the jump rope. How can I get him more used to it?

Try putting the jump rope on the table and under the dog before asking him to jump. That way, he will get used to seeing it under him. Don't use any big motions when using the jump rope to start out with. Small motions work best, and you can do fuller turns as your dog becomes more comfortable with the rope.

46

Fetch A Drink

Teach Your Dog To Bring You A Drink When You Ask For It!

Difficulty •••••••••••••••••••••••••••••••••• Moderate
Prerequisite •••••••••••••••••••••••••• Take It, Bring It, Give
Items Needed •••••••••••••••••••••• Clicker, Treats, Soda Bottle

Whether you're reclining on the couch watching a football game or just sitting around with friends, this can be a useful—as well as entertaining—trick for your dog to know. It can also be a fun game for your dog, and once he's learned it he may not want to stop! Just be sure to have a handkerchief ready to wipe down that drink (or tell him to "Bring a tissue," Trick #47). If you have guests over, a good idea is to be very casual when showing off this trick. Nonchalantly say to your dog, "I'm thirsty Max, bring me a drink." When he comes back, open it up, and continue your conversation with your guests. They should be just as surprised as you are pleased.

Step 1: Get a bottle of soda appropriate for your dog's size and put it on the ground. Tell your dog to "Take it." Click and treat when he does. Do this several times.

Step 2: Now, tell your dog to "Take it" and "Bring it." When he brings it to you, tell him "Give" Do this repeatedly and remember to click/treat.

Step 3: Put the bottle a bit further away from you each time. Only click and treat if he takes it, brings it, and drops it into your hands. Soon, you can eliminate the three commands and instead use the phrase, "Bring me a drink!"

Step 4: Try asking him to perform the trick from different spots in the room, and then move to different rooms.

OUR EXPERIENCE

When I taught Caspian this trick, I used a 16.9 oz. bottle of Dr. Pepper. That's a pretty big bottle, but I thought he could handle it because he's so big. After a little encouragement, Caspian started knocking over the bottle and picking it up with his mouth. We had to teach him to first knock it over, then pick it up—he was getting frustrated by trying to pick it up. He was also scared of the full bottle, either because of the weight, or because of the imbalance of it sloshing around. We decided to completely empty the bottle to begin with, then fill it gradually as he continually completed the trick. I would tell him to "Take it," and "Bring it." This took him a while to get the first time. I gave him a big jackpot when he did, and took a break from training. In the next session, after some review, this time I would say "Bring me a drink." Each time I had him do it, I would put the drink in a different spot, just a little bit farther away from me. Soon, whenever I told him to "Bring me a drink," he would run into the kitchen, grab a drink by the fridge, run back with it in his mouth, and then drop it in my hand!

TEACHING TROUBLE

Why can't he pick up the bottle?

Caspian learned to knock the bottle over with his nose or paw, and then pick it up with his mouth. Just be quiet when your dog seems to get frustrated and don't try to prod him. Dogs are smart; they'll figure out what they need to do.

It's too heavy for him!

It may not be. That's what I thought when I was teaching Caspian this trick, so I emptied the soda bottle. Of course, he picked it up fine. I kept clicking and treating when he would take it, and while he was eating his treat, I filled the bottle up little by little with water. Soon, the bottle was filled up all the way to the top, and Caspian picked it up just fine. He was just not used to carrying something that heavy in his mouth, but after we worked on it, he didn't have any trouble.

> **TIP:** *"If you're having trouble getting your dog to pick up the drink bottle, try getting him to first learn to knock the bottle over before trying to pick it up."*

47

Bring A Tissue

Teach Your Dog To Bring A Tissue, And Then Discard It

Difficulty ••••••••••••••••••••••••••••••••	Moderate
Prerequisite ••••••••••••••••••••••••	Take It, Bring It, Give
Items Needed ••••••	Clicker, Treats, Box of Tissues, Waste-basket

This is a great trick to do immediately after Trick #46, "Fetch a drink." After your dog brings you a drink, you can then ask him to bring you a tissue to wipe down the bottle. After learning this trick, you dog should be able to carefully pull out a single tissue, bring it to you, and then throw it away in the garbage bin. This is an incredible trick on its own, but paired with "Fetch a drink," it makes quite the show-stopper.

The First Part: Bring a Tissue

Step 1: Set a tissue box on the ground. Tell your dog to "Take it." He may want to take the whole box - but when he takes one tissue from the box and pulls it out, click and treat.

Step 2: Have him continue to do this until he starts pulling them out on his own. Then, have him "Bring it" to you and "Give." Click and treat.

Step 3: Continue to do this until he does all three commands without hesitation. Start saying, "Bring me a tissue" when he drops it in your hand.

The Second Part: Throw It Away

Step 1: Get out your waste basket. Give the tissue back to the dog and have him "Bring it" to the waste basket and "Drop it" in. Click and treat.

Step 2: Keep doing this until he takes it, brings it, and drops it without problems or hesitating. Then, use the command "Throw it away" while he is dropping it in.

Step 3: Continue to practice this, just saying "Throw it away" instead of the three other commands, until he is able to throw away the tissue at your command.

TIP: *"Just so you know, you're teaching your dog to pull out all the tissues from the tissue box! Make sure he can't get to them when you're away from home."*

OUR EXPERIENCE

This trick wasn't difficult for Caspian to learn. First, I showed him the tissue box and touched the tissue. "Take it," I said. He pulled one out. I clicked and treated. I did this again. And again! But the next time I had him "Take it" and "Bring it" to me. When he had brought it to me, I told him to "Drop it" in my hand. When he dropped it, he received a big treat! We did this several times until he knew exactly what to do.

In another session, we worked on throwing the tissue away. I had him bring me a tissue. Then, I "used it" and gave it back to him. Pointing towards the trash can, I told him to "Drop it." I clicked and treated. The next time he did it, I used the "Throw it away" command. Soon, Caspian was able to bring me a tissue, and then take it back and throw it away in the trash!

TEACHING TROUBLE

He won't pull out the tissue!

Try pointing to it and say, "Take it." If that doesn't work, encourage any good behavior that is close to what you want. If he touch-

es the tissue, click and treat. Then say, "Take it." He'll probably understand.

He pulls out the tissue fine, but then he wants to throw it away before he gives it to me!

If he does that, don't click and treat. Before he drops it in, say - "No - Bring it!" He'll then bring it to you. Soon, he'll remember to bring it to you every time.

48

Turn On/Off A Lightswitch

Teach Your Dog To Switch A Light On And Off

Difficulty •••••••••••••••••••••••••••••••••••• Hard
Prerequisite ••••••••••••••••••••••••••••••••• None
Items Needed •••••••• Clicker, Treats, Touchstick or Laser Pointer

This trick assumes that your dog is tall enough to reach a light switch when he jumps up to the wall. If you have a smaller dog, you can still do the trick, but will need a table or other platform for your dog to stand on while jumping up to reach the switch. I used a laser pointer to attract my dog to the lightswitch, but if you don't have a laser pointer, that's okay, the touchstick will work just as well. If you do use a laser pointer, make sure that it is a low wattage model, and keep it away from your dog's eyes. There are two parts to this trick: teaching your dog to turn on a light, and then teaching him to turn it off again.

The First Part: Turn On A Light:

Step 1: Using either a laser pointer or touchstick, get your dog in the habit of jumping up to touch the light switch. It is best to have him jump up with his pads on the wall (instead of his claws)

touching the switch with his nose. I used a laser pointer here, because I would play with it as a game, knowing that he would really go after it even if it's on a wall.

Step 2: Using the clicker, begin clicking only when his nose pushes the light into the 'on' position. He will begin to realize the effect of his action, and expect a treat after the light comes on.

Step 3: Begin to only click when your dog begins and ends the trick by successfully turning the light on. He needs to understand that the trick is not two parts (jumping up on the wall, and hitting the switch) but one.

The Second Part: Turn Off A Light:

Step 1: The first step is very similar to step one of teaching him to turn 'on' the light. Get your dog used to jumping up on the wall, but instead of his pads touching the wall, click when his paw hits the light switch.

Step 2: Begin clicking only when he successfully turns 'off' the light switch. Dogs will notice the change in light in the room, and will usually look expectantly when he successfully turns out the lights.

Step 3: Begin clicking only when your dog successfully completes the trick from beginning to end. He needs to learn that in order to be treated, he has to perform the trick in one session.

OUR EXPERIENCE

When I taught this trick, I used a laser pointer to get Caspian to jump up on the wall. Caspian loves to chase the laser around, and will drop everything to try to catch it. He now will even go after reflections and glints of light off of lamps, glasses, and other shiny objects. Because he gets excited like this, I thought it would be a good way to get him to do something that he wouldn't normally do.

> **TIP:** *"Laser pointers are often a great way to motivate and excite your dog. It can also act as a reward."*

TEACHING TROUBLE

My dog keeps tearing up my wall!

To turn off the light, dogs are unable to do this with their nose, and must use their paw. Because of this, it is incredibly easy to receive scratch marks and torn wallpaper. If you use this trick a lot, you might want to consider installing clear Plexiglas around your light switch.

49

Teach Your Dog Limp

Teach Your Dog To Limp On Command

Difficulty •••••••••••••••••••••••••••••••••••••• Hard
Prerequisite •••••••••••••••••••••••••••••••••••• None
Items Needed •••••••••••••••••••••••• Clicker, Treats, Leash

This very well may be one of the hardest tricks to teach your dog, and is one many movie dogs learn and act out on the silver screen. Next to "Jump Rope" and "Bang," it doesn't get much harder than this. Although teaching this trick can be frustrating at times, it is a momentous achievement once your dog learns it, and can bring joy and laughter to you and your family, not to mention guests and friends.

Step 1: Hook up your dog's leash to his collar and use it to pull his front dominant paw up - be very careful as you walk with him - click and treat when he walks one or two steps.

Step 2: Keep doing this until he is successfully 'Limping' with the help of the leash.

Step 3: Try to encourage your dog to put less weight on his lifted paw. Over time use less and less force on the leash, and he will be able to limp on his own.

OUR EXPERIENCE

Teaching Caspian to limp was very frustrating at times. It took a lot of work, many training sessions, a whole bag full of treats, and many many hours. But it was well worth it. After teaching your dog this trick you can combine it with "Crawl" and "Play Dead" to give your guests a thrilling death scene (See Trick #52, "Bang"). I started out by attaching his leash to his collar, and using it to support his paw, keeping it in the air. Then I held my clicker away, motioning him to walk to it. I clicked and treated as soon as he made a couple of steps forward. The downside to supporting his paw in this way is that it may condition him to put more weight on that paw, the opposite of what you want. There are other methods you can try such as putting a sock on the paw. Usually dogs will try to raise that paw, feeling the unbalance. Whichever method you use, be consistent, but don't feel like you can't try new things if your dog just isn't getting it. When teaching this trick, keep in mind that teaching your dog to limp on command is one of the hardest things to do, so be patient, be consistent, and vary the reward.

> **TIP:** *"Be patient! This trick can take months to perfect; don't rush it. Dogs learning this trick need several breaks because of the stress you're putting on his mind and body."*

TEACHING TROUBLE

He won't transition into lifting his paw on his own!

It may take a long time for your dog to understand what he needs to do. It takes a long time of determined work to get this trick, even if you have a smart dog. Keep working with him until he gets it right!

50

Teach Your Dog Crawl

Use This Trick To Get Your Dog To Crawl Towards You

The dog jumps over trenches and dodges humming bullets. The mud is blanketed with a sheet of barbed wire fence, mangled from explosions. He must escape the raining bullets, the thundering explosions. He drops to his belly and crawls underneath the barbed wire. Bullets fly and dent the ground. Clumps of dirt and rock cling to his fur. He crawls, scratches his muzzle on a barb, but still crawls. Crawls to safety.

Whether or not your dog is a movie dog like this one, crawl is an easy trick that yours should know. With it, you can teach all sorts of other tricks—as well as teach him to navigate obstacle courses and other tricks and games. Teaching this trick will also pave the way for teaching "Bang" (Trick #52).

Step 1: Tell your dog to lie down.

Step 2: With treat in hand, coax your dog to move forward with the touchstick. Make sure he does so while in the down position.

Step 3: Repeat several times. Once your dog is crawling naturally, begin saying "Crawl" before you click and treat.

Step 4: Try stepping back from your dog and giving him the command, "Crawl." Click and jackpot if he responds to "Crawl." If not, revert to previous steps.

OUR EXPERIENCE

Teaching Caspian to crawl was one of the first tricks we did when he was a puppy. I remember the very first trick we taught him was "Touch," touching the touchstick on command. The next tricks we taught him were "Sit" and "Down." And, I believe, the trick that we taught after that was crawl. We wanted to put his new-found knowledge of the touchstick to good use. Even though he was a puppy, and extremely prone to becoming distracted, he was able to learn this cute trick in only a few training sessions. We first had him lie down. We put the touchstick right in front of him and asked him to touch. I'm sure we expected him to crawl to the touchstick, but that's not what he did. Crawling is hard, so he jumped to his feet to touch the stick.

We compensated and the next time, positioned the touchstick only an inch in front of his nose. As he was lying there in the down position, he stretched forward to touch the stick. We clicked and gave him a really good treat.

We continued this method, and gradually moved the touchstick further and further from him. Each time, he would inch forward, and before long, he was crawling to get the touchstick.

TEACHING TROUBLE

Help! My dog won't crawl forward to get the treat, but gets up from his "Down" position.

Don't give him the treat if this happens. This is a trick where you have to exercise patience, and don't get too excited! If you act excited, your dog will get excited too. Make sure you have a great treat to lure and give him commands in low tones. If you have to, you can keep a hand on his body to discourage him from getting up.

TIP: *"Use this for dance routines, funny comedy sketches, or to retrieve something in a cramped place too small for a human."*

51

Teaching Play Dead

Your Dog Rolls On His Back And Lies Still

Difficulty •••••••••••••••••••••••••••••••••••••• Moderate
Prerequisite •••••••••••••••••••••••••••••••••••• Down, Touch
Items Needed •••••••••••••••••••••••••••• Clicker, Treats, Touchstick

This is a famous trick that many dog owners teach their dogs. There are two ways to teach this trick: the first is by catching the behavior with the clicker. Many dogs lay on their backs, especially if they're looking for a belly rub. If you notice your dog doing this often, click this behavior and then associate the action with the command, "Play dead." The second way of teaching this trick is by using the touchstick to shape your dog's behavior. This method is outlined below. "Play dead" is a fun trick to teach, and can be used in conjunction with "Limp" and "Crawl" for the "Bang" performance (Trick #52).

Step 1: Have your dog lie down. Take your touchstick, or with your treat in hand, slowly guide it so that your dog moves into the "Play dead" position. Click and treat. Repeat until he gets into the "Play dead" position without help from the touchstick.

Step 2: Keep repeating the process while saying, "Play dead!" See if he'll do it at your command.

Step 3: In different training sessions, shape and perfect the trick by only clicking when he is in the exact position you want him to be in (i.e., legs in the air, paws bent, unmoving, etc.).

OUR EXPERIENCE

When I taught Caspian this trick, I started by having him lie down. I slowly moved the touchstick saying softly, "Touch," from one side of his head to the other side to get him to roll onto his back. When he got onto his back, I clicked and treated. I repeated this several times until he understood that he had to roll onto his back to get his treat. I stopped using the touchstick at this point and instead used a hand signal (hold first three fingers out, rotating hand around) as he did his trick each time. At this point, I got picky. I would only treat if he was in the exact position I wanted, with his paws bent and his legs sticking up in the air. Each time he did this, I would click and treat, saying my command, "Play dead" until he could respond to my command.

> **TIP:** *"Combine this trick with "Limp" and "Crawl" for the "Bang" performance!"*

TEACHING TROUBLE

He stands up to touch the stick rather than roll over to do it.

This part of the training process depends on you. Be very gentle in your movements and commands. Keep the touchstick close to his nose and within his reach. You want him moving slowly to touch it. If you are slow and determined in your actions, your dog will be as well.

52

The Bang! Performance

Teach Your Dog This Showstopper Death Scene Performance!

Difficulty ••••••••••••••••••••••••••••••••••••••	Hard
Prerequisite •••••••••••••••••••••••••	Limp, Crawl, Play Dead
Items Needed ••••••••••••••••••••••••••••••••	Clicker, Treats

Great work! You've made it to the final trick. Your dog has mastered the basics now, moved on to harder and more advanced ones, and now you're ready to attempt "Bang," the final, hardest, most extraordinary trick combination in this book. Now don't get discouraged before you even begin—it's not going to be easy, it will take a lot of work to master, but this is the single best showstopper that's sure to leave your friends speechless. Your dog must be incredibly smart to have made it this far, and now he's just one trick away from knowing all 52. You can do it! Don't stop now!

A dog shows its teeth and growls, staring unblinking into a gun barrel. He stands protectively before its wounded master lying on the floor of a wet ally.

It charges towards the gun. A muzzle-flash bolts in every direction. A lead bullet whisks through the air and strikes home. The dog stops in shock and its teeth fades from view.

It limps, retreating from the gunman. It trips to the ground and crawls, crawls to its master. It reaches his side and whines. Rolls on its back, belly upturned, then is still.

A moment's pause. A voice in the sky authoritative and commanding deep and resonate over all things: "CUT" it says. Everything around flips with action, speeding movements in a whirlwind of excitement. The voice speaks again: "Check the gate."

The dog jumps to its paws and looks around, panting. A man chants over a headset to a person invisible. He pets the dog and feeds it a large treat. "Good boy, Max!" he says, "Get ready for the next take, buddy."

Step 1: Tell your dog to "Limp," "Crawl," and "Play Dead," clicking and treating after he performs each action.

Step 2: Now, give him all three commands again, this time keeping the treat until the end. Repeat several times.

Step 3: Now say "BANG!" before giving the three commands and while he is in his "Play dead" position. Click and treat.

Step 4: Continue to practice this, eventually getting rid of your three initial commands so that he does all three together as soon as he hears "BANG!"

OUR EXPERIENCE

The biggest challenge here is the individual tricks themselves. Caspian had to be well-acquainted with each of the individual tricks, and so we began by drilling them over and over again. The hardest one of these, by far, was limp. Once he was able to perform this consistently, we began to string them together. Once you have the individual tricks down, putting them together isn't as much of a challenge. However, repetition is key, and if you're working on a trick such as "Bang" as a performance trick for your next barbecue, make sure you drill it over and over again in different parts of the house. We found that Caspian can perform a trick perfectly in one room—but if we try it in a different part of the house, he has trouble. When teaching tricks such as this one, teach in a wide variety of places. Be creative: maybe train some at a local dog park. If your dog can perform amidst all the distractions and interesting things going on around him, you've been highly successful.

> **TIP:** *"You could also add 'Speak' as a yelp of pain to make the demonstration even more thrilling!"*

TEACHING TROUBLE

My dog will respond, but it takes him too long to get it.

Work with your dog to obey you right as you give this command for a great performance. But if your dog is too excited when you want to show him off, you can still make things fun. If he doesn't respond to "Bang" right away, just shrug and say, "So sometimes I'm not that great of a shot."

Final Thoughts

CONGRATULATIONS! You've finished all 52 tricks! It is quite an accomplishment for your dog to know so many tricks, and that's a reward in and of itself. The time you've spent with your dog has strengthened your friendship with him. With each new trick you build trust and companionship, as well as memories for the future.

We hope you have enjoyed these tricks as much as we have, and we hope that your work with your dog doesn't end here.

For more training tips and tricks, visit our website: www.doggiebuddy.com.

Or follow us on Facebook or Twitter:

www.facebook.com/doggiebuddy
www.twitter.com/doggiebuddy

Printed in Great Britain
by Amazon